SCHOOLING *through* TRAVEL

How the World Became Our Children's Classroom

TARYN ASH

Created and published through Taryn Ash Enterprises.

Copyright 2018 Taryn Ash

Printed in the United States of America

All Rights Reserved. No part of this text may be reproduced, stored in a retrieval system, or transmitted by any means, electronic, mechanical, photocopying, desktop publishing, recording, or otherwise, without permission from the publisher. No patent liability is assumed with respect to the use of the information contained herein. While every precaution has been taken in the preparation of this book, the publisher and author assume no responsibility for errors or omissions. Neither is any liability assumed for damages resulting from the use of the information contained herein.

All terms mentioned in this book that are known to be trademarks, registered trademarks, or service marks have been appropriately capitalized and are denoted with a (R), a TM or an SM. The publisher cannot attest to the accuracy of this information. Use of a term in this book should not be regarded as affecting the validity of any registered trademark, trademark, or service mark.

What You'll Find Inside

Taryn Ash and her husband, Sam, spent eight months exploring 12 countries on four continents with their 7th and 8th-grade children. While working hands-on to rehabilitate monkeys and baboons, tending to a wounded black rhino in the South African bush, studying Buddhist meditation in rural Laos, and teaching English to children in Zimbabwe, the kids still managed to complete a year's math curriculum in a third of the time normally required, research articles about HIV/AIDS in sub-Saharan Africa, and interview people trying to save a coral reef on a remote island in the Philippines. While their family explored New Zealand by campervan, their kids learned about black holes, thermal energy and seismology. They danced with San Bush people and attended a Herero tribal wedding in Namibia, and did restoration work on a medieval house in France, all while working their way through stacks of classic novels and non-fiction accounts of the places they were visiting.

This book is a practical guide for traveling parents who seek strategies for teaching math, science, English and social studies to their own children on the road, while taking full advantage of the tremendous learning opportunities that travel provides. In these pages you'll find practical advice on the entire process, as well as sample assignments and suggestions for educational activities for all age groups.

In writing this book, Taryn drew from her 25-years of experience as an award-winning curriculum designer, college lecturer, high school teacher and stakeholder in a tutoring center.

Dedicated to my wonderfully supportive husband, Sam, and our precious children, Declan and Scout – the best travel partners I could have ever wished for.

Table of Contents
Schooling-Through-Travel

Chapter 1: Introduction 1

Chapter 2: Getting School Approval 11

Chapter 3: The Schooling Through Travel Process 23

Chapter 4: Learning Supplies & Resources 35

Chapter 5: English & Social Studies - Reading 43

Chapter 6: English & Social Studies - Writing 49

Chapter 7: Math 75

Chapter 8: Science 79

Chapter 9: Assessment 87

Chapter 10: The Resistant Child 95

Chapter 11: The Post-Tour Report 103

Conclusion 117

About the Author 119

Also Featured in this Book 121

Another Book by Taryn Ash 123

RHINO RESCUE - Travel Journal Entry (unedited)
by Scout Ash-Dale (age 12)
Limpopo, South Africa
April, 2016

"Ok, guys, our mission is back on." Emma, our game ranger, said after knocking on our door.

We knew what this meant because a couple hours before, we were told we were going to help vets with an infected eyed rhino. We had all gotten ready quickly... perhaps too quickly because we ended up waiting for five minutes, then ten minutes, then a half an hour, then we all said forget it, the pathetic rhino can wait.

We had to wait because a helicopter was supposed to arrive to pick up the tranquilizer gun so that the rhino could be found and put to sleep, but times got mixed up and we all went back to our Sunday off.

"Great! We're ready!" Mom replied. "Scout, go get your father in the lounge area."

I nodded and dashed off to alert him. Well, I didn't run because one isn't supposed to run in Africa, especially in a reserve with the Big 5, so instead I sped walked.

"Hello." I said to my Dad sitting in an armchair. "We have to go save a rhino!"

"Holy strawberries, what?" He said. Only he didn't say strawberries.

"A black rhino has an infected eye so its about to be tranquilized so the wound can be dressed. We have to help." I replied.

Dad got up and walked to the room.

After about ten to fifteen minutes of being bounced around like popcorn in a Land Rover, we arrived at a small clearing with the sound of a whirring helicopter above. Emma, who was driving, listened to a static message on the walky-talky.

"The rhino has been tranquilized." She said to her passengers in the back. These included me, my family, two young Swiss-German ladies, Corrine and Felicia, and one 82-year old Swiss-German man, George.

Emma started the jeep again and drove down a dirt rode and stopped in the middle, bushes on either side of it. There was already a flashy SUV parked in front of us. Out emerged two women whom I thought to be vets. One of them opened up the back and called us over. We all stood in line waiting to be handed something to carry. She handed my brother a rope, my dad a box, and me a plastic bucket with an orange cattle prod inside.

"Don't touch it!" She advised.

Wow, thanks for telling me. I was just about to see if I could fit it in my mouth.

Once everybody had something in their hands, Emma started through the bush... running. So we all followed... running. After five minutes of running through thorns, we arrived at a clearing with an enormous female black rhino. There was a towel over it's eyes and three vets surrounding it.

After a few medical inspections and applying antibiotics, the male vet with a broken back from a previous rhino attack turned to us volunteers. "I'll give you five minutes to pack up and get out of here." He said.

"You wanna bet? I can do it in three." I thought.

So all of us started to pack up our things and run. I scanned the ground for my orange weapon, the cattle prod and found it lying on the ground out of its bucket. I picked it up by the handle as people who were sprinting by me started to respect my personal space. I glanced around for the bucket and found it being carried by one of the swiss ladies, Felicia. "I need that bucket." I said quickly to her.

"Vas?" She asked.

"I need that bucket." I repeated, pointed to what she was carrying.

"Va . . ." she began, but I grabbed the bucket out of her hand and ran before she could say "hot sausage".

We began running as quickly as we could through bush, dodging low lying branches and thorns. The William Tell Overture was playing in my head.

The nurse that gave me the cattle prod was standing next to a tree yelling, "Faster! Faster! One minute until the rhino wakes up!"

"What?" I thought. "The rhino is going to wake up? Aaaaahhhh!"

The classical music in my head was replaced by rock n' roll and I started to run through bushes and not around.

After three minutes of running through bush, we arrived at the road again.

"I did it!" I thought. "I made it in three!"

We all climbed back onto the Land Rover and sighed tired sighs when we heard that Nick, the rhino tracker, was still in the bush, up a tree.

Chapter 1
INTRODUCTION

It was on a train from Toyama to Nagoya, Japan, where I began hatching my plan. I had just completed a one-year teaching contract at Toyama Minami High School, where I led classes in English and international studies. Now, I was off to catch a flight to Singapore to begin a new job as a college lecturer of communication. I don't recall what the exact catalyst was, but I spent the entirety of that four-hour train journey immersed in my thoughts about flexible ways of educating children, in stark contrast to the highly-formalized system I had just come from. And more precisely, I was working out how I would homeschool my own kids one day. This wasn't going to happen right away - heck, I didn't even have a boyfriend at the time - but I was consumed by the idea of teaching my kids differently - better - and I carried those musings with me for the next twenty years.

Every day while living in that coastal Japanese city, I spotted compelling learning opportunities to share with my students. But the system wasn't set up for that. My role as a guest teacher was to stick to the highly-regimented class format that was being echoed in every high school from the north of Hokkaido, right down to the southern-most tip of Okinawa. There was little-to-no room for the experiential learning I craved for them.

I still recall some of the diagrams I drew up and notes jotted down, on those loose pieces of paper spread out across the small table in front of me; plans of how I would combine structured math and science curricula with a more adaptable approach to English, foreign languages, social studies and the arts. Essentially, the idea was that my role as the parent would be to consciously place my children in situations where learning would not only happen, but would lead to an ever-increasing appetite for more. It wasn't about test-taking or memorizing arbitrary facts, comparing students against each other or measurable standards. What I had in mind was the antithesis of repetitive, teacher-driven, desk-bound, textbook-dominated classroom learning. I wanted to create conditions in which my children's intellectual curiosity and potential would blossom out in the world, by harnessing all of their senses.

I met my future husband and father of my children, Sam, six weeks-to-the-day after boarding that train, and twenty years later, we made the decision together to put our conventional lives on hold, pull our two kids out of school, and head off to explore the world. Our journey began in South-East Asia, then on to New Zealand, to multiple locations in Africa and finally, Europe. Every step along the way turned into an adventure. It was big, life-changing and, without a doubt, the smartest thing we ever did as parents. And it was fun . . . so much fun.

That around-the-world journey finally gave me the chance to school the kids while we traveled, and realize my dream of teaching them as I had envisioned on that train those many years earlier. The results were profound - the kids thrived, they learned far more than we could have anticipated, and they enjoyed it. We all did.

The specifics of our journey are described in my previous book, **GRAB THE KIDS & GO: A Practical Guide to Our Family's Gap Year**, whereas this book concentrates on only one aspect of that experience - how we approached our kids' schooling while traveling.

This topic is of particular interest to many parents I have spoken with. It's no surprise that they baulk at the thought of schooling their children while traveling. *We already struggle to get the kids to do their homework at home, how are we possibly going to keep them disciplined on a beach in Fiji?* Other concerns revolve around getting permission from the children's school to let them out to travel for several months. And then, once permission is granted, *What are you going to teach?*

Despite these worries, schooling our children while traveling around the world was a good decision. Change that. It was the *best* decision. We all got so much more out of our world tour *because* we included schooling in the mix, as it forced each of us to be far more conscious of what we were experiencing than had we been on a standard family vacation.

Our daughter, Scout, was 12, and Declan was 13 and turned 14 while we were traveling. Most of their learning assignments focused on where we were at the time. Their exercises required them to explore the streets with their eyes wide open, taking deliberate note of everything that was happening around them, truly talking with people, asking questions and reflecting on what they were taking in.

Sam and I pushed ourselves to research every location on our itinerary more deeply because we wanted to be able to answer the children's questions satisfactorily and, almost more importantly, ask them thought-provoking questions that might raise their awareness about what they were witnessing and experiencing.

A brief confession

Straight up, I should let you know that I came at this with a bit of experience. For many years of my professional life, I worked as a training consultant developing and running award-winning learning programs for professionals in the workplace. I already mentioned above how I briefly taught high school in Japan, before becoming a college lecturer. And I continue to be a stakeholder in a tutoring center in China. To top it off, I homeschooled our daughter for a few months when we first moved to Houston. For all these reasons, I developed our children's *schooling-through-travel* curriculum with a fair amount of confidence that it would work. And it did!

What I hope you do not take from this is that you need a background in education to make this process work. Rather, I hope that you borrow from our experiences, and perhaps those of other educators in your life, to develop a program that suits you and your family. I have provided real assignment examples and strategies for you to launch from, and I predict once you get started, interesting and fulfilling learning opportunities will reveal themselves with increasing regularity. At that point, your question will shift from *What can we teach?* to *Which of these amazing learning opportunities should we choose?*

BEACH BUNGALOW ESSAY WRITING, WITH A COMPUTER ON HER LAP & KINDLE UNDER HER SEAT.
PHILIPPINES

2 TAKEAWAYS

1. Schooling your kids on the road does not need to detract from your vacation experience. In fact, it can add a heightened awareness and curiosity about the places you're visiting that is not always present on a standard family vacation.

2. You don't need to have a background in education for the schooling-though-travel system to work for you.

Chapter 2
GETTING SCHOOL APPROVAL

One of our bigger hurdles to overcome before the trip, was getting approval from our kids' school in Houston to allow them to be absent for several months. Sam and I were well aware that there were few places available at their private school, and there was no guarantee that ones would be held open for our two the following year. So, I prepared our *pitch* carefully, by anticipating what the school decision-makers cared most about, what concerns they might have about our taking the kids away for several months, and what messages they would need to hear to be won over.

The following pages summarize our own unique experience in getting school approval. How this might compare with yours is impossible to predict, but it might give you an idea of how to begin.

Begin with the end in mind

Begin the schooling-through-travel process by answering these two questions:

- *Am I fine with my child returning to her current grade level after the trip?*
- *Would I rather that my child learns enough while travelling to move up a grade when she returns to school?*

If you decide that staying in her current grade is the right decision, then you will have significantly greater freedom to choose what will be studied during your travels. You can simply choose learning activities that appeal to your family's values and your child's interests, without worrying about meeting the criteria set by a specific school system. This option may be a perfectly sound one for those parents who are not confident that they, or their child, will stick to a structured learning plan. Moreover, I have met families who held their kids back a year in order to travel, and the results have generally been positive. Upon their return, the kids compared well against their younger classmates, and their grades and academic confidence improved noticeably.

One such family chose to hold their 16-year old son back for one academic year while they explored India. He had been going through a bit of a rough patch at school - slacking off and not getting the results he would eventually need to get into university. So, they held him back and started the academic year over again six months later. This break, plus the insights he gained from traveling, seemed to be the catalysts he needed to get his act together. He applied himself more when he returned to school, and his grades shot up. Within a year and a half, he was accepted into his university of choice. To this day, his parents tell me that decision was one of the smarter ones they made for their son.

Holding our two kids back, however, was not an option, simply because they didn't want it. Both Declan and Scout liked the idea of studying while on the road so they could move up a grade when they returned. In fact, the thought of it appealed to them. They looked forward to finally reading books of their choosing, exploring topics of interest to them, and indulging their creativity, rather than spending the same year sitting at a desk learning about the world through the pages of a textbook.

Who's responsible?

From the outset, Sam and I agreed that having one parent primarily responsible for the schooling process made things simpler and more streamlined. It became my responsibility to make sure that the curriculum would achieve our agreed goals, which were a combination of the school's requirements and our personal ideas about what the children should learn. It was also my job to keep track of the kids' progress during the trip. Actual teaching was split between Sam and me, according to our strengths and interests. Sam taught geometry, physical geography, general science and some writing, and I covered the remaining math, social studies and English topics.

Approaching the school

In preparation for our meeting with the school administrators, I bounced my ideas around with a handful of Canadian educators I knew, to get their opinions about my learning strategy. All five private school admissions officers and three public school teachers I spoke with agreed that a comprehensive portfolio of work completed while traveling, plus satisfactory completion of an accredited math program, should be ample to move them into the next grade. It came as such a relief to hear that these seasoned educators shared our family's view that international travel can be an excellent substitute for traditional schooling.

Emboldened by this positive input, I drew up a comprehensive plan that listed what each of our children would cover in math, science, social studies, English - writing and reading - and the few extracurricular activities we had already planned. An outline of this was then presented to the school's admissions officer who, once convinced that our plan was a sound one, arranged for a formal meeting with the middle and high school principals.

Initially, I was terribly nervous that a "no" response would dampen our enthusiasm for the trip. By the time the meeting rolled around, however, our travel itinerary was being formalized behind the scenes at such a pace that we knew that the school's response would not determine whether or not we went. Sam and I walked into that meeting with a quiet understanding that, regardless of the principals' answers, we were going. Our son would be entering high school the following year and we saw this as our last chance to travel the world as a family without disrupting those critical pre-university school years. If the school chose not to accept the kids back, the backup plan was for me to homeschool them until an alternative solution was found upon our return.

The learning plan

Below is the learning plan that I presented to Declan's high school administrators. (I created a similar plan for Scout that differed only in what would be covered in math and science.)

Essentially, each child would be required to complete six research assignments during our eight-month journey, plus produce a journal entry or creative writing story based in each location. They would examine social, political, historical or economic topics, or more likely, a combination of these. As you will see, the media through which they conveyed their learning were varied and flexible. (More on that in following chapters.) We also wanted to make sure that they came away with some essential knowledge about each country, plus basic language vocabulary and demographic facts. The book list was chosen to complement our travel itinerary.

I did not include specific details about what would be covered in math because we based it on the standard US curriculum according to grade level. I simply stated that Declan would complete 8th-grade Pre-Algebra. The science topics were drawn directly from the school's curricula that he would be missing while we were away.

LEARNING PLAN
Declan Ash-Dale

SOCIAL STUDIES & ENGLISH

Suggested essay topics:

Vietnam

- Based on your visits to sites throughout the country, and supplementary reading, write an *article* explaining what you learned about the Vietnamese perspective of the American-Vietnam war.

Laos

Choose one of the following:

- Write an *essay* describing how Buddhism is practiced in Laos.
- Produce a *documentary* on life in rural Laos.

New Zealand

- Develop a tourism promotion *brochure* that covers at least five New Zealand sites.

Philippines

- Interview students and teachers at a Philippine village school and develop an *essay* or *documentary* comparing and contrasting that schooling experience with your own.

Zimbabwe

- Either individually or as a team, produce a *video documentary* on your community volunteer work in Zimbabwe.

Namibia

- Develop a **_PowerPoint presentation_** or **_brochure_** on self-driving tours of Namibia, including wildlife, landscapes and culture.

South Africa

Choose one of the following:

- Either individually or as a team, produce a **_video_** or **_essay_** on the work of the Bambelela Wildlife Sanctuary.
- Either individually or as a team, produce a **_video_** or **_essay_** on the Siyafunda Conservation Program.

France

Choose one of the following:

- Produce an **_article_** about the history of the French village, Roquecor.
- Write a **_personal essay_** on your impressions about what you learned about D-Day while in Normandy.

Creative Writing & Journaling

For each country visited, choose one of the following options (minimum 1000 words):

- Write a creative story based in the country, drawing from your experiences, observations and reading.
- Write a non-fiction account of one of your experiences in the country.

- Write a non-fiction piece on an aspect of the country's cultural, historical or political situation.

Country Fact Sheet

For each country visited, develop a *Country Facts Sheet* including:

- Language(s) spoken
- Currency
- Population size
- Main ethnic groups
- Top industries
- Literacy rates
- Average income
- Top five tourist sites
- An interesting fact worth remembering

For each country visited, learn how to say these phrases in the local language:

- *Hello*
- *1,2,3,4,5*
- *Goodbye*
- *How much? (cost?)*
- *Thank you*

(Note that these facts will be added to the **Family Trivia Game.**)

Reading

Choose six books from the list below, or nominate alternative books to be agreed with your parents.

- *Into Thin Air* by Jon Krakauer
- *I am Malala* by Malala Yousafzai
- *The Boy who Harnessed the Wind* by William Kamkwamba & Bryan Mealer
- *Born Free* by Joy Adamson
- *A Long Walk to Water* by Linda Sue Park
- *Elephant Whisperer* by Lawrence Anthony & Graham Spence
- *Nightingale* by Kristin Hannah

MATH

Complete 8th-grade Pre-Algebra

SCIENCE

Learn the basic principles/features of:

Chemistry

- The Atom
- Elements, compounds and mixtures
- Formulas

Physics

- Force and motion

- Gravity
- Waves
- Transfer and conversion of energy
- Specific heat
- Kinetic and potential energy

Astronomy
- Basic theories

More of a suggestion than a commitment

Despite our having a well-thought-out curriculum for each child, we never required, or expected, or even desired that it would be followed to the letter. Rather, the plan gave us a basic structure to follow. Global adventures are by their very natures unpredictable and, of course, that meant that we were in no position to predict what we were going to see, or do, or learn. The educational opportunities would only present themselves once we were on the ground. Thus, we approached the study plan as more of a suggestion than a commitment. We were more than willing to have the original assignment ideas superseded by more appealing ones that presented themselves along the way. Some of the assignments were fine-tuned, and others were entirely replaced. In fact, as you will see in Chapter 11: *The Post-Tour Report*, the kids produced more work, and read far more, than what was proposed in the original learning plan described above.

Permission granted

As it turned out, our children's school administrators were receptive to our plans, agreed that the kids would benefit enormously from our tour, and accepted the proposed curricula. Their only proviso was that each child would need to sit a math placement test before the beginning of the next school year to confirm that they had the necessary prerequisites. It was also agreed that both children would present their academic portfolios to a select group of teachers at the beginning of the new school year. I was delighted with this idea, as I saw it as an ideal way to motivate Scout and Declan to take their learning projects seriously.

Disclaimer

- *Getting school approval depends largely on your own school district and administrators. What is described here is simply our experience. There may be school policies or legal restrictions in your area that limit your ability to take kids out of school for an extended period. I suggest researching this well before making your travel plans.*

5 TAKEAWAYS

1. Begin with the end in mind. Decide whether your child will move up a grade level at the end of your travels, or if he will stay in his current grade. Your decision will fundamentally determine what content will need to be covered.

2. Agree between the adults involved *who will be responsible for what. Who will lead the process? Who will design the assignments? Who will keep track of work completed? Who will tutor the kids in specific subjects?*

3. Design a learning plan that is agreeable to all stakeholders – the child, the parent(s), and the school administrators.

4. Do not expect, or require, or even desire, that your learning plan be followed precisely. It is meant to provide a basic structure and possible options. Valuable learning opportunities that present themselves on the road should be allowed to supersede your original ideas.

5. Be honest with yourself about whether you are prepared to put the necessary time and effort into teaching your child while traveling. If the answer is no, consider your options. (Some of these will be touched on in Chapter 4: *Learning Supplies & Resources*.)

Chapter 3
THE SCHOOLING-THROUGH-TRAVEL APPROACH

Schooling our kids while traveling was a genuine pleasure, although in many ways we didn't teach so much as *facilitated* their learning. Our role was to regularly place them in new and different worlds and then assist in opening their senses to what was happening around them. As facilitators, we assigned projects that would help them absorb those experiences more deeply and consciously.

The aim of the schooling-through-travel methodology is to educate, not to evaluate. Our kids were coming from a school system plagued by a *teach-to-the-test* philosophy that stresses grades before actual understanding. Our objective was quite the opposite – for our kids to develop a greater appreciation of the world, and a craving to learn more about it.

My schooling-through-travel approach is entirely customized to the interests, needs, and abilities of the child, and wherever possible, the projects are linked to the locations visited.

SAM, DECLAN & ETHAN (OUR FELLOW-VOLUNTEER) HAULING WATER TO THE GARDEN OF SUFFERERS OF HIV/AIDS, ZIMBABWE

As part of our family's community service work in Zimbabwe, for instance, we spent time helping in a garden for people living with HIV/AIDS. As the days progressed, we met more and more people who had been directly affected by this health crisis that for decades has enveloped Sub-Saharan Africa. Some of the children we taught English to had been orphaned by the disease, and a startling number of adults we met had taken in children of their deceased relatives.

It was in that context that 14-year old Declan began research for his paper entitled *Zimbabwe's Struggle with HIV/AIDS*. He supplemented his observations and interviews with data he had found on the internet. With each passing day, he became more aware of, and more sensitive to, the devastating impact of the disease, and he turned his learning into a solid, insightful piece of research work.

Similarly, 12-year old Scout produced an entertaining and informative video on the Bambelela Monkey Rehabilitation Sanctuary where we volunteered for two action-packed weeks. Through a combination of video, photos and narration, she produced an informative seven-minute movie that led the audience through the stages of the rehabilitation process, from when the monkeys enter the facility to when they are finally released back into the wild. The final product proved, to an almost startling degree, how much she had learned in such a short period, not only about the rehabilitation process but also about primate behavior and social order, as well as wildlife conservation in general.

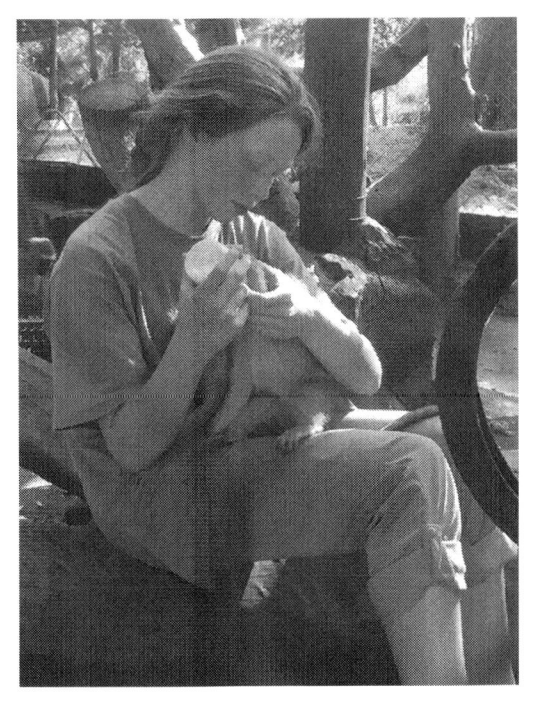

*FEEDING BABY MONKEYS WAS A DAILY ROUTINE AT BAMABELA.
SOUTH AFRICA*

We successfully used this schooling-through-travel approach in social studies, English, and sciences like physical geography, meteorology, environmental science and wildlife studies. Math and some other science topics were taught using educational resources that will be described in coming chapters.

THE PORTFOLIO

The focal point of the schooling-through-travel process is the portfolio, which could be a digital and/or physical file containing the evidence of the child's learning experiences and projects. For our traveling youngsters, this included a variety of:

- Essays
- Articles (in a style appropriate for newspapers or magazines)
- Journal entries
- Documentary-style videos
- PowerPoint presentations
- Creative writing stories
- Reviews of tourist activities on *Trip Advisor*
- Lists of books read
- Outlines of online courses completed

If we were to do it again, I would add:

- Personal blogs
- Online writing contests (which can be found by searching *kids/teens online writing contests*)
- Recorded interviews with experts in the field

For younger children, I would use the following learning methods:

- Drawings and paintings of their experiences and observations
- Comic strips showing sequences of events
- Fiction and non-fiction books the kids write and illustrate themselves
- Stories told through song, dance or acting (recorded)
- Descriptive letters or emails to family and friends

- Captioned photographs
- Recorded interviews with family members about shared experiences
- Videoed conversations with memorable persons met while traveling
- Labeled collections of postcards, currencies, stamps, brochures and admission tickets

Kids' Tech Skills

Don't underestimate the potential IT skills of your kids! I know many children as young as five and six-years old who can do basic PowerPoint and movie editing, cutting and pasting still photos, adding music and narration. Take it from me, in no time at all your young ones may be teaching YOU how to use your own technology.

Portfolios for Younger Kids

Seth and Alison, both teachers, had their daughters produce a physical portfolio following their trip to India.

"Both of our daughters, ages 6 and 9, kept a journal and wrote in it each day. It helped them process all the things we were doing and the people we were meeting, and they were excited about doing the things in anticipation of recording it in their journals!

The very day we returned, they started a scrapbook of the trip. I had ordered one beforehand and it was waiting for us. The memories were fresh, we got to revisit all the great things we did and talk about them, and could do so in a more concrete, tangible way than just going through pictures on the computer.

When their friends come over and ask about the trip, they pull out the scrapbook and show them, and they are able to remember all parts of the trip. They tore out the pages of their travel journal and pasted them in the scrapbook to the corresponding pictures to give the complete feel of the trip."

CAMILA AND AVRA'S PORTFOLIO, AGES 6 AND 9

A Sample of Our Learning Experiences

These might give you an idea of the many types of experiences that can be turned into thought-provoking learning projects.

- A private tour of a Vietnamese wholesale water-market, rice and noodle factory
- A class in cooking Lao cuisine (including local market tour)
- Kiteboarding lessons, Philippines
- A lesson in Hmong weaving and rural family life, Laos
- A food tasting tour of Vietnamese local restaurants, where we ate cobra and crocodile
- A personal tutorial in Lao Buddhism and monastic life by a senior monk
- An informal lesson in how to climb coconut trees and pick mangoes, Philippines
- A tour of war sites and Vietnamese-American war museums, Vietnam
- An underground caving tour to view glow-worms in New Zealand
- A tour of a New Zealand's volcano museum and activity center
- A sea kayak tour of New Zealand's unique flora and fauna
- A privately guided introduction to a Ndebele tribal village, Zimbabwe
- A presentation on how to stay safe on a Big Five wildlife reserve, South Africa

- Talks with elderly residents of a community home about their fascinating lives, Zimbabwe
- Lessons in traditional hunting and gathering methods of San Bush villagers, Namibia
- Discussions with anti-poaching activists, South Africa
- Hands-on animal rehabilitation work, South Africa
- A privately guided introduction to a Himba tribe, Namibia
- Learning games taught by local children, Philippines and Namibia
- Collecting wildlife data for academic research, South Africa
- Wildlife viewing in Etosha National Park, Namibia.
- A presentation and demonstration by an anti-poaching squad, South Africa
- Visits to ancient Catholic monasteries and churches
- Spanish language lessons taught by the owner of a local café
- Restoration work on a French medieval house and garden wall
- Regular visits to French gourmet outdoor markets
- Visits to impressionist galleries
- Attendance at a regional medieval festival set in an ancient castle

DECLAN SHARING A LAUGH WITH A SAN
HUNTER AND MEDICINE MAN.
NAMIBIA

The portfolio's uses

The portfolio creates a focal point for the child's studies – a permanent archive of their learning experiences.

For our kids, the portfolios showcased to their teachers the wide range of learning they had gone through. The content could also be used in future academic projects and college entry applications. In her freshman year at high school, for instance, Scout used an essay she had written about teaching in Zimbabwe as the basis of an analytical essay she was assigned in English class. She didn't copy the original assignment, but drew ideas from it.

More personally, our family's memories will forever be archived in these portfolios. Several of the kids' writing projects and artworks have been pasted into our family vacation albums, and the videos are being held on files that can be watched and shared forever.

TRACKING PROGRESS

I can't stress enough how important it is to keep track of your child's study progress, otherwise the credibility of the entire process can unravel. *If he thinks you're not really going to insist that he complete his work, then why would he bother trying?*

There may well be software applications to help you do this, but I found that a simple table for each child's work was sufficient for daily updates. We used the data to create a report to be presented to the school administrators when we got back. (See Chapter 12: *Post-Tour Report*)

Remain flexible

For a number of reasons, including not having dependable WIFI available on occasion, we had to adopt a flexible attitude about what could be accomplished from one day to the next. Some evenings the kids would put in an hour on one subject after dinner and 30 minutes reading before bedtime. Other days, often when it was rainy, cold, or we were simply tired of sightseeing, the kids would put in a staggering 3 or 4 hours doing a wide range of subjects, or make serious progress in a single one. Occasionally, we would skip studying all together, although we tried to avoid this as much as possible because, for this process to work, and to reduce the kids' resistance, we needed them to adopt studying into their daily routines.

Study Tracking Table

Date	Math	Science	Social Studies	Reading	Writing	Extracurricular
January 9	Reached 12% mastery of Pre-Algebra	Plate tectonics - basics		Born Free (to page 53)		
January 10	Reached 13% mastery of Pre-Algebra	Plate tectonics review			Wrote journal about ceramic village	Visited ceramic village, Saigon
January 11						
January 12	Reached 19% mastery of Pre-Algebra	Plate tectonics quiz			Wrote journal about cooking class	
January 14		Volcanoes - introduction	Essay on Vietnamese Food - first draft	Born Free (to page 76)		Visited water market, Can Tho

4 TAKEAWAYS

1. Your role as the study-through-travel facilitator requires you to intentionally place your child in situations where she will see and experience new things. Align your learning plan to these situations, matched to the learning needs, abilities and interests of the child.

2. In an easily-updateable working document, track your child's work in each subject.

3. Hold all of your child's completed project work in a digital or physical portfolio.

4. Don't feel the need to stick too tightly to a specific time schedule since you can't always predict where you will be or what you will want to do at any given time. First and foremost, you're on holiday, so don't let the studying overshadow everything else.

Chapter 4
LEARNING SUPPLIES & RESOURCES

Gone are the days when students need to pack heavy textbooks and files for every class. Online tools and ebooks allow traveling families the freedom to carry little and still have easy access to a huge variety of first-rate learning resources.

In the back of a tuk tuk with our carry-on sized backpacks.
Laos

TRAVEL SCHOOL SUPPLIES

Just weeks before departure, each family member received a new carry-on sized backpack for Christmas. The design included a protective front-pouch ideal for a laptop computer and other school supplies – a Kindle (ebook), writing and drawing paper pads, as well as pencils and pens. For photos and video recording, Scout brought her phone and Declan his compact camera. Each child also had earbuds for listening to audiobooks and online videos (of the educational variety). That was all we needed.

Laptop Computers

To take full advantage of the marvelous online learning resources available, each of our two kids brought their own laptops. Math and science were done almost exclusively online. Project research was conducted through the web, while documentaries and PowerPoint presentations, creative stories and academic papers were all produced on these computers.

The original plan was that the kids would upload their assignments on their own web pages or blogs, but access to WIFI varied too much from place to place for this to work. So, we changed course and simply had them save a copy of each assignment in their own digital files, a second copy on my laptop, a third on a memory stick, and a final copy was held in *iCloud*. Was so much caution overkill? Perhaps, but I had heard horror stories from friends and family who had lost their devices while traveling and their photos along with them. Computers can be broken or stolen, and how dependable is the Cloud, anyway? Even the staff at our local Apple store in Houston suggested we keep a backup, just in case. So, we did!

No computer games

Sam and I felt strongly that this world tour was our chance to get the kids away from computer games, and that their computers would be used solely for schooling. To our surprise and delight, we did not get the major push-back that we expected, even from our son who usually preferred to play computer games above all else. Declan was told months before departure that he was not going to be playing computer games while we were traveling because they would be a constant distraction to him, and he accepted it without much complaint.

What we had learned from years of travel with our son was that if he knew that at the end of the day he could play his favorite computer games, his mind would drift to those games even while we were doing amazing things in exotic places. He would constantly try to wrangle more computer time into our precious holidays. He would sneak onto the computer when we weren't looking, and we would have to spend our time policing him to make sure he got off when he was meant to. It was a major pain that had no place on this tour. So, we made it a non-issue by eliminating games from both kids' computers entirely.

OK, we did make one compromise. Sam installed a small number of games onto his old iPad, exclusively for use on airplane flights. We took 15 flights over the course of our tour, and not all airlines guarantee in-flight entertainment. So, we relented and allowed games for *flights only*, which meant that Declan actually anticipated the grueling 23-hour flight between Houston and Singapore with enthusiasm.

Note that this No Computer Games (except on flights) policy requires a firm commitment by both parents. From our experience, if one parent flinches the whole system can fall apart. I know plenty of parents who have caved, saying that they would only allow games to be played in restaurants or after long days of touring. But we found that those were the times when some of our family's best conversations took place. We all grew fond of evening reading times and family card games after busy days of touring and found no good reason to give those special times over to screens.

WIFI Access

One of the greatest challenges we faced once the trip was underway was gaining access to dependable internet service. Our chosen math and science curricula required WIFI, but as availability was inconsistent from country to country, town to town, hotel to hotel. What we found surprising was which countries had easily accessible internet and which did not.

We found that even remote villages in Laos, one of the poorest countries on the planet, had high speed, free, internet service. The kids could easily study in any hotel, guesthouse room or café, which turned out to be a blessing since we arrived unprepared, and under-dressed, in Luang Prabang in the middle of the worst cold spell in the region's recent history. The weather made it the ideal time for the kids to stay inside and make serious progress in their studies. This turned out to be a wise move as WIFI access in our next location, New Zealand, was far less consistent and more expensive. *Who would have guessed?*

We had a campervan booked for three of our four weeks in New Zealand and had purposefully booked spots at some higher-end campsites to be sure to have internet access. Although all the sites claimed to have WIFI, each had a different system for charging fees for the service, depending on the amount of data or length of time used. It turned out to be expensive, and meant rushing off to the reception desk day and night to get updated passwords when the old ones had expired. To make matters even more frustrating, the quality of the WIFI was often weak so the kids spent too much valuable study time waiting for data to upload.

In the end, we could not predict where we would have dependable WIFI so we made sure to take full advantage of it when it was running well. When it was not available, the kids focused on writing, reading and drawing.

Ebooks

The world of ebooks has made reading while traveling a breeze. They are light and easily portable, and new books can be added wherever WIFI is available.

Each of our family members received a *Kindle Paperwhite E-Reader* for Christmas just before the tour began. We had used Kindles for years but decided to splurge on the Whitepaper version for the trip because it can be read in any lighting - in tents and campervans, on airplanes, on beaches and when we were up all night with jetlag, without disturbing others.

Care was taken to make sure the Kindles were always charged and new books downloaded whenever high-speed internet was found. (Note that ebooks only require WIFI to download books, not to read them.) We also took advantage of the excellent free book options found through *Kindle Unlimited.*

Kindle allowed us to share books amongst ourselves, which helped us save a bit of money. More importantly, we could read books concurrently and then discuss them.

Audiobooks

Audiobooks turned out to be superb learning and entertainment resources for our family, as I will explain in more detail in Chapter 5: *English & Social Studies - Reading.* If you choose to use audiobooks, remember to bring along quality earbuds for each user, and if your device has poor quality sound, a small portable speaker.

ONLINE RESOURCES

These days, traveling parents have a wide variety of online options and tools at their disposal, making schooling on the road increasingly feasible. What proportion of your learning plan will be based on these online resources is a decision you'll need to make.

My resistance to choosing a complete online curriculum – for math and science, as well as social studies and English - simply came down to wanting the kids to focus, as much as possible, on where we were traveling at the time. Studying a prescribed social studies and English curricula would have meant focusing on places, histories and literature unrelated to where we were traveling, which we felt would have defeated the purpose of schooling while traveling. We certainly did not want our children distracted by studying US history while we were working on restoring a medieval house in France, for instance. *Would it not make more sense to learn about the life of a 15th-century French peasant?*

Although the kids did tap into online resources to conduct research for social studies, English and science, the only actual online curriculum they followed was for math - the details of which are covered in Chapter 9: *Math*.

Online curricula options

Not all parents want to put as much time and personalized attention into customizing their child's curricula as we did. Many are perfectly satisfied, if not relieved, to have a prescribed set of assignments, reading lists, schedules and assessments for their child to follow. That makes sense, and might be the wisest decision for your family.

To work out whether available programs match your needs can be as easy as conducting a standard internet search, starting by typing in *homeschooling programs*. Beyond the commercial programs available, your local or federal government may provide resources for homeschooling families.

As you research your options, ask yourself questions like:

- *Does this curriculum match the work our child will be missing at school?*
- *Would we prefer a program that has a set schedule, including specific start, end, assignment and assessment dates, feeling that it might provide the structure our child needs?*
- *Would we prefer the course's schedule be entirely flexible, allowing our child to work and break when it's most convenient?*
- *Would we like our child to have access to a professional tutor who can be communicated with via email, Skype or telephone? Or, are we confident enough in our own academic abilities and discipline to support our child through the course?*
- *Would we prefer a course that exclusively uses online resources, or would we be prepared to carry textbooks or other schooling materials along with us?*
- *Would we prefer a program that provides some form of certification upon completion? Or, would evidence of completion, such as Khan Academy's Mastery designation, be sufficient?*
- *Would we prefer a free or fee-paying program?*
- *How easy would it be to cancel the program, if we were not satisfied? Is there a money back guarantee?*

5 TAKEAWAYS

1. Plan your child's school supplies carefully so they don't weigh you down. Remember to pack pens, pencils, drawing and writing pads, an ebook, earbuds, a camera device, and perhaps, a laptop computer.

2. Work out your own views on whether to allow electronic entertainment on the trip, by considering how it might impact your child's study habits and your time together.

3. Expect WIFI access to be inconsistent, and therefore be ready with alternative study assignments that don't require it.

4. Upload audiobooks for study and entertainment. Remember to bring earbuds and/or a small speaker.

5. Explore online learning resources before departure, and remember to pack supporting materials and necessary electronic devices. (And don't forget backup chargers and cables!)

Chapter 5
ENGLISH & SOCIAL STUDIES
- READING

Our kids read books throughout the trip that complemented our travel itinerary. Most, but not all, were non-fiction stories that contained elements of history, culture, and wildlife of the locations we were visiting.

Weeks before landing in Africa, we had begun reading about it. I still recall our shared thrill of driving along the long dirt road through the Makalali Wildlife Reserve on our first day, spotting things that we had read about. Giant termite mounds looked exactly as we had imagine them. Equally exciting was the sight of entire trees uprooted and crushed along our path. *Was that caused by elephants?* we asked the driver. *Yes, it was!* Only because we had all just read *The Elephant Whisperer*, by Lawrence Anthony, could we spot those signs.

Reading became our family's nightly pastime. We would discuss books in pairs or as a group, and then the kids would combine their real-life experiences with what they had read to produce a variety of non-fiction and creative writing works.

Combining English & Social Studies

Essentially, English and social studies were taught as a single, inclusive subject. Most of what the kids read taught them aspects of history, geography and the social sciences of the places we were visiting. Their writing assignments – be they non-fiction or creative writing – focused on those same topic areas. This proved to be the ideal way to have both subjects covered, and in half the time.

BOOKS

At certain points during the trip the kids were reading as much as a book a week, which was far more than what they could manage during the regular school year. Part of this was due to the extra time they were afforded to read, but it was also because they were also finally given the chance to choose books of genuine interest to them. I dare say that far too often the books assigned at school did not appeal to our kids, which made reading a tiresome chore. I had reason to believe that they were skipping whole sections of their assigned reading just to get through it, but that was not the case when the kids chose their own books. Although we did provide a suggested booklist, they choose several additional ones themselves.

Despite our 12-year-old daughter being in Honors English at school, we worried that she did not challenge herself when choosing books for pleasure. She chose ones that she could get through quickly and easily, on subjects already familiar to her. This changed as soon as we set off on the tour. It was exciting to watch her open up to new authors and subjects.

Being the animal lover that she is, she began with two books about wildlife in Africa. Both *Born Free* by Joy Adamson and *The Elephant Whisperer*, as mentioned above, utterly captured her imagination, and she completed them in no time flat. We all followed her lead and read the books ourselves.

Once in Africa, we all moved on to humorous books by Peter Allison, about his life as an African safari guide - *Whatever you do, don't run! True Tales of a Botswana Safari Guide*, and *Don't Look Behind You! A Safari Guide's Encounters with Ravenous Lions, Stampeding Elephants, and Lovesick Rhinos*. Not highbrow literature, to be sure, but they were wonderful books to share because there were so many parallels between his adventures and our own.

Scout also read *The Martian*, by Andy Weir, recommended to her by her big brother. Science fiction was new to her and she enjoyed the story immensely, leading to interesting conversations between the kids. Sam also read the book and then led a "book club" session between the three of them in our New Zealand campervan. They critically examined the content and author's writing style, just as one might do in a college seminar. The kids were up for the challenge and there's no doubt that they got a lot out of the exercise.

Perhaps the most useful advice I can offer with regards to reading is to schedule in a regular "reading time," when all distractions are turned off. We created a nightly routine of making ourselves comfortable, and reading together either silently or aloud. We would discuss what we read, the kids would ask questions about vocabulary and content, and it turned into a special part of our time together. In no time at all, reading became a welcome substitute for screens.

CAMPFIRE KINDLE-READING,
NEW ZEALAND

AUDIO BOOKS

Audiobooks were included in our routine for variety, but the benefits were greater than that. Listening to well-read stories turned out to be an excellent way to share books as a family, especially on long drives and during lazy evenings when we all preferred to listen rather than read.

Sometimes kids just want to be contrary, like when our two refused to read any of the Harry Potter books, despite my pleading... or, perhaps, because of it. Finally, during a grueling multi-day drive through the Namib Desert, I convinced them to listen to *Harry Potter & the Sorcerer's Stone*, superbly narrated by Jim Dale. This was a trip perfectly suited to Sam and me because the landscape was spectacular and like nothing we had seen before, but the hours of gravel roads and dunes would have been pure misery for the kids had it not been for that 20-plus hour audiobook. As soon as the first book of the series was ended, they began the next one, and by the time we flew out of Africa they had listened enthusiastically to the first five books in the series and were keen to continue through the rest.

To audiobook or not to audiobook?

No doubt there are parents out there who think that listening to an audiobook rather than reading is somehow *cheating*. I used to feel that way until I learned that professional educators recommend audiobooks for improving children's listening comprehension. When Declan was younger, although he had no problem with the mechanics of reading, he struggled with fully understanding what he read. Sometimes he missed key details or lost his way through storylines. In response, we began having him read while listening to audiobooks. The strategy of using both senses – sight and sound - at the same time worked almost immediately, his comprehension improved enormously, and reading soon became a pleasurable activity for our boy.

Other beneficiaries of audiobooks are individuals with attention deficit disorders who find sitting and reading for extended periods a serious challenge. With audiobooks, they can move around freely while still listening.

Audiobooks can be pitched a bit higher than what the child might be used to, and may contain more challenging themes and language. That said, we used the pause button liberally to confirm that our kids understood what was going on in the stories before moving on, particularly in convoluted Agatha Christy mystery novels, which our family particularly enjoyed.

When Scout was 10, I homeschooled her for five months, until a space opened up at her chosen school. During that time, whenever we traveled by car, we listened to books and educational podcasts. She particularly enjoyed listening to the *Famous Five* series of children's novels, so one of her assignments was to write her own mystery story in the style of Enid Blyton, the series' author. It turned out to be a genuinely successful project because, as she explained it to me, she could hear the characters' animated British accents in her head, just as she had heard in the recordings. These voices inspired colorful and imaginative dialogue like she had never produced before. Her final product was a lengthy and highly entertaining 11-chapter novel.

Similarly, during our gap year, Scout, now 12, chose to write a multi-chapter story in the style of *Anne of Green Gables*' author L.M. Montgomery. Once again, her writing took on a voice and direction that flowed onto the page.

What these exercises proved to me is that we don't exclusively learn to write through what we read; we can also learn to write through what we hear.

5 TAKEAWAYS

1. Choose books that match the locations you're traveling in and, in this way, pair your child's English studies with lessons in social studies.

2. Think carefully about the books your child reads on the tour - challenging but accessible, entertaining but educational. Encourage your child's love of learning by giving him a say in which books he reads.

3. Download audiobooks that educate as well as entertain. Some of these might be good for your whole family to listen to together.

4. Create a daily reading routine that works with your family's rhythm.

5. For variety in your child's writing assignments, encourage him to borrow from the writing styles of different books and audiobooks he enjoys.

Chapter 6
ENGLISH & SOCIAL STUDIES
- WRITING

Writing was an ever-present activity for all of us during our family gap year. Sam returned to his roots as a journalist, blending his reflections of our experiences with his extensive knowledge about world history and politics. Declan had long been a creative storyteller, first in detailed comic strips throughout his primary school years, and eventually graduating to captivating short stories. His interest in writing simply flourished while we traveled. Scout, who had always been a strong academic writer, blossomed as a creative writer once she had the time and freedom to do so. And I showed a new level of discipline in updating my travel journal daily, eventually turning my attention toward writing this series of books for traveling families. The fact that we were all writing, and regularly sharing our efforts with each other, created a momentum in all of us to keep it up.

Finding the time & space to write

We found that days too hot to venture out to the beach were ideal for writing for an hour or so in a hammock under swaying palms, as were evenings in our cozy campervan, and after a full day of hiking and kayaking. It was wonderful how many idyllic places we found that inspired us to write. Cafes were always a possibility, of course. We also wrote in our tents, grass huts and next to blazing campfires.

Oh, and yes, those seemingly-frustrating WIFI-blackout periods, which limited what other studies could be done, were perfect times to simply settle in and write, and write.

The kids' writing took three forms: travel journaling, creative writing and assigned non-fiction writing.

CREATIVE WRITING & JOURNALING

Group writing

Creative writing became a pleasurable pastime for the kids pretty early on in the tour, beginning on our third evening of travels, in Ho Chi Minh City (aka Saigon). The kids convinced me to take them for a foot massage, so we rolled up to the first day spa we found and went in.

So many details of the experience at the spa were hilarious to us, from the faint sewage odor, to the grimy lukewarm water our feet were washed in, to the elegant South-east Asian ladies slapping our legs and feet with burning hot stones, and then contorting our legs high above our heads. It was a unique cultural adventure worthy of remembering, so we remained silent on the subject until we arrived back at the hotel to write about it from our own unique perspectives. We then read our compositions aloud and it was so funny to hear how differently we interpreted that shared experience. From then on, we relished the chance to write and entertain each other with our stories.

On our last day in South Africa, a rare black rhino needed to be treated by a veterinarian for an eye injury. This required the vet to be helicoptered to the location where the animal was last seen and to tranquilize it from the air. Our group, including Declan and Scout, had to make its way through the bush at high speed with medical supplies to where the rhino finally collapsed. Following the treatment, and with the helicopter still flying overhead to keep predators at bay, we high-tailed it out of the area before the groggy rhino woke up. We were told that if it smelt us it would give chase and we would have to climb the nearest tree or termite mound.

That was the most intrepid thing any of us had ever done. And what a great tale! Once again, rather than sharing our stories immediately, we returned to the camp and each cozied into our bunks to write the story from our own perspectives, to be shared aloud over dinner, and kept for posterity in our family's travel album. (Scout's story opens this book.)

Writing improves writing

By the end of our eight-month tour, 12-year old Scout had written over 15,000 words in creative writing, and Declan an astounding 25,000 words, about half of which were contained in a science fiction novel he wrote entitled *Andromeda*. In every case, the kids chose to write these stories for their own entertainment, and we found that the quality of the work improved to a startling degree from week to week.

*SCOUT MAKING FRIENDS WITH TWO HIMBA GIRLS OF A SIMILAR AGE.
NAMIBIA*

Avoid editing creative writing & journals

Aside from occasional suggestions about information that might be added for posterity, Sam and I chose *not* to edit the kids' journals or creative writing. Those activities were meant to be entirely personal and pleasurable. I suspect that is why the kids never hesitated to share their creative works with us.

The more the kids read and wrote, the better they got at spotting their own errors, and grammar mistakes became fewer and farther between. Where we did make a point of giving feedback was on their academic work.

ACADEMIC WRITING

The children produced at least one non-fiction project in each country visited, which could be a:

- Research essay
- Article
- PowerPoint presentation (including voiceover)
- Brochure or promotional flyer
- Video documentary

For a list of assignments what might be more suitable for a younger child, see Chapter 3: *The Schooling-Through-Travel Approach*, in the section *The Portfolio*.

Sample writing assignments

You have already read about some of the assignments our children completed during the trip. Here are a few more examples. Most of the assignment ideas came from me, although the kids were welcome to suggest their own ideas or modify my ones.

English & Social Studies - Writing

1. *Write a research essay on the challenges in protecting a coral reef in the Philippines.*

The idea for this project came to us after weeks of quietly living on a secluded island just a couple of hours boat ride from Boracay. Every morning and evening we would borrow a small, wooden fishing canoe and paddle a few meters out over the coral reef located just outside our huts, to snorkel in the crystal-clear water. It did not take long for us to grow fond, almost possessive, of that reef and the abundant tropical fish who lived there. Gradually, over the course of a few days, we noticed that local fishermen were paddling closer and closer, until finally they were catching fish directly from the reef, despite it officially being a protected area. Our collective outrage turned into a valuable learning opportunity.

Scout interviewed individuals in the area to get their perspectives on the situation. She spoke with business people who were concerned that a depletion of fish from the reef would impact the tourist trade they were hoping to build. She also talked to local fishermen who struggled to feed their families on the meager catch available around the island. She learned how fishermen in the area who tried to support their families on less than $5.00 a day knew of only one other option to fishing - piracy. And she heard from local investors about efforts underway to find employment alternatives for the fishermen so they would leave the reef alone.

This turned out to be an important research project for our 12-year old because her opinion evolved over time as she began to understand the different perspectives of those involved. It was a story about environmental conservation, economics, politics and human survival.

EXPLORING "OUR REEF",
PHILIPPINES

2. *Develop a PowerPoint presentation on the Vietnam-American War from the Vietnamese perspective.*

Both children developed essays on the Vietnamese-American War from the Vietnamese point of view, which were then turned into narrated PowerPoint presentations.

To begin the process, Sam and I taught them what we knew about the war from the American perspective, using some additional sources we found online and in our guide books. Most Westerners will have heard the anti-Communist American version, and we were no exceptions to that, so it was eye-opening for all of us to hear the positions put forth by the ruling Vietnamese Communist party, presented in Vietnamese museums, and from average people we spoke with who lived through the conflict.

This gave our kids the chance to understand a well-known historical event from the point of view of the *other side*. It challenged perceived truths about the war, and provided a unique opportunity to show our kids that history is subjective, observed through the lens of the storyteller.

KEEPING THE SUN OFF, VIETNAMESE- STYLE

3. *Write a first-person account of life as a Lao monk.*

    While exploring the Lao village of Muang Ngoi, we came across a tiny Buddhist temple inhabited by a senior monk and his three novices. To our delight, we were invited inside and spent a few precious hours being instructed in Buddhist chant and meditation, and told fascinating stories about monastic life in rural Laos. This was one of the real highlights of our world tour. So as not to forget what we had learned, the kids each wrote a 1000-word first-person account of life as a Lao monk.

    Requiring it to be written in the first person – *"I am a monk who ..."* - added an interesting twist to the exercise. It challenged

55

them to develop a deeper level of empathy with their protagonists. Part of their assignment was to include details we had been taught about monastic life, so it also served as a form of journal. Once the text was written and edited, the kids added photos and inserted it into newsletter format they amusingly entitled *Monk Weekly*.

MUANG-NGOI, LAOS

4. *Develop a brochure promoting six adventures we experienced in New Zealand, using all five senses in your descriptions.*

This project turned out well, especially for Scout who had been lacking confidence in her descriptive writing. She knew how to write to get good grades at school, but held back on using her imagination to its fullest. By focusing on what she saw, heard, smelt, touched and tasted, her prose came alive. She began taking risks with her use of metaphor and simile.

In time, we discovered that our daughter had turned this thinking process into a creative game that she played even outside of her writing. She would compose vivid descriptions of her environment in her mind while snorkeling, rafting or lying on the beach. And this practice showed through in her increasingly vibrant writing.

ENJOYING SENSORY OVERLOAD,
NEW ZEALAND

5. *Argue that science fiction is a valuable literary genre, using examples from each of the sci-fi books you have read.*

Our son read several science fiction novels during the early months of the trip. We could have encouraged him to vary his reading choices, but he had long been a hesitant reader and his comprehension needed work, so we were thoroughly delighted to see him devour those sci-fi classics, as it was just what we felt he needed to develop a passion for reading.

Rather than having him write a paper on each book, we determined that the greater benefit would come from learning how to structure and develop an academic argument paper; skills he would increasingly need in high school and university. This was our chance to coach him using literature he genuinely enjoyed.

Sam took on the project and, admittedly, it proved to be a taxing one for both of them. But it was also highly valuable. They spent hours working on it in our beach hut in the Philippines, when it was too hot to go outside. By the time they had finished, Declan had a much clearer understanding of what a good academic paper should look like, and the steps he needed to get there. It was only when we read through his subsequent essays, that we realized how much learning had indeed resulted from this assignment.

6. *Critically examine the English teaching program we worked with in Zimbabwe. What were its strengths, how could it be improved?*

Doing community service in Zimbabwe was one of the real highlights of our journey. Much of our time was spent teaching English at an orphanage and a variety of schools in and around Victoria Falls.

While Sam focused on building and maintenance projects, the kids and I helped run English language classes for pre- and primary school children. We, and a couple of other college students, developed learning activities. Once in the classrooms, all of us, including Scout and Declan, led class and small group activities.

Scout took to teaching like a duck to water and was coming up with some surprisingly mature insights about how to improve the classes. This led to her writing an essay on the strengths and weaknesses of this particular English teaching program. As I do have an education and curriculum design background, the two of us had a wonderful time together talking about learning objectives and ways of engaging the children. It was clear that as she worked through the essay her level of observation and awareness increased considerably, and her insights became more astute.

SCOUT TEACHING ENGLISH PHONETICS TO ENTHUSIASTIC PRE-SCHOOLERS. ZIMBABWE

Types of essays

To help you come up with assignment ideas for your child, here are brief descriptions of four essay types commonly taught in schools. Give your child the freedom to choose from a range of media through which to communicate her ideas. (See media options listed in *The Portfolio,* in Chapter 3.)

1. Through the **narrative essay**, your child ***tells a story*** to the reader.

   During virtually every day of your trip, your child will experience novel situations that he can write about. It could be a story about what happened over an entire day, or simply a brief moment worth remembering. Allow your child to communicate in the first person, using "I" throughout. This kind of story should build toward a conclusion or personal statement.

   Personally, I feel that this is the most accessible format for any age group. A younger child may not be able to write a narrative essay *per se*, but he may be able to tell his story in a recorded interview, a letter to his aunt back home or in a picture he had painted that he then describes to you through conversation.

   Here are examples of prompts a parent could suggest:

   - *What happened the moment I met a bear in a Canadian forest.*
   - *How I learned to carry buckets of water on my head, like African women do.*
   - *While sailing around Australia, I decided not to jump into the clear blue ocean. Here's why.*
   - *The day I became a good bargainer, at the Yashow Market in Beijing.*
   - *The scariest thing that happened to me in the Amazon jungle.*
   - *My huge wipe-out while boogie boarding in Bali.*

   Note that this book opens with a narrative essay written by our daughter, describing our adventure with a black rhino.

2. Through the **descriptive essay**, your child *paints a picture* for the reader.

   The process of describing a thing, an event or a feeling requires your child to concentrate on the details, and use expressive language.

   We found that encouraging our children to use all of their senses – smell, taste, touch, sight and sound - to imagine their stories brought their works alive.

   An older child may choose to write these words out in essay format and then record a narrated video or PowerPoint presentation. A younger child may express her ideas in words that are then translated into a painting or picture book.

   Here are the types of prompts you might use to encourage your child to write a descriptive work:
   - *The sights and smells of Istanbul's Grand Bazaar*
   - *What it's like to snorkel over a coral reef in Australia*
   - *The thrill of alpine skiing*
   - *Different types of bathrooms I experienced in China*
   - *My favorite things to eat at an outdoor market in France*
   - *The beautifully-dressed ladies of Rajasthan*

3. In the **expository essay**, your child provides the reader with *facts*.

   Expository essays are often characterized by cause and effect, compare and contrast, and "how to". They require facts, not feelings or emotions, and is not to be written in the first person.

   Based on our experience, this type of assignment is more accessible to older kids, and teens in particular. If nothing else, they might find the process more interesting than a younger child would. But that is not to say that you can't find topics that will appeal to your younger ones; just know that they might require more parental involvement in the writing process.

For instance, your younger child may describe the animals in a zoo you visited, including the number of each species, how they were being housed and cared for, and the foods you saw them being fed. She could then compare that with what she has witnessed at your city zoo back home.

Declan wrote two expository essays while we were in Africa, which could also have been turned into a video documentary, an article for his school newspaper or a blog post.

- *How Zimbabwe is tackling the problem of HIV/AIDS*
- *Anti-Rhino Poaching Efforts in the Limpopo region of South Africa*

Another topic he considered was *How drought is impacting communities in Southern Africa*.

Examples of prompts for expository essays might include:

- *How schools in the US differ from the one we visited in Peru*
- *How Laos has been dealing with its massive landmine problem*
- *How Sri Lankan cuisine compares with England's*

4. The **persuasive essay** is meant to ***convince the reader*** to accept the writer's point of view or recommendation. The writer uses facts and logic, as well as examples and expert opinions, to build her case. She should also present the other sides of the argument, while putting forth a convincing reason why her position is the right one.

   This is a challenging style of essay, but it can be a great way to motivate a child to express himself.

I recall this being the case when Declan was disturbed by the abuse of elephants we witnessed in Laos' tourism industry. In reaction, he wrote a persuasive review on *Trip Advisor*. It didn't take long before he began receiving appreciative responses from other tourists whom he convinced not to visit those tourist sites. It proved to be an excellent opportunity for our son to learn how writing can have real-world impact.

For your younger child, she might begin by listing her views on why a farm stay in Scotland makes for an excellent family vacation. Then, she could be interviewed by her sibling on camera to share her opinions and providing examples from her personal experiences.

Prompts for a persuasive essay might include:

- *It's easier to learn Spanish in a Spanish-speaking country than in a classroom.*
- *Volunteering is the ideal way to learn about African wildlife.*
- *The tourism industry is harming Tibetan communities and culture.*
- *The best way to travel through Europe is by train.*

WRITING ASSIGNMENT PROMPTS

Younger kids

- "Draw a picture of the market we visited and label the different foods and activities we saw there."
- "Make a storybook/fairy tale about the castle we visited today. Draw pictures."

- "Update our family's Facebook page with a description of the pottery class we took today. Include captioned photos of the class and the cups we made."
- "Research facts about an animal we saw, and display what you learned on a small poster. Include photos we took."
- "Record an interview with your sister about what she found interesting/funny/different at the museum."
- "Write a story entitled "Why I would like to be a wildlife ranger", including facts that you learned on the safari."
- "Write a letter to Grandma and Grandpa about the game your new Nepali friends taught you."

Ages 10 – 12

- "Create a PowerPoint presentation on the dishes we made at the cooking class. Include photos and recipes."
- "Draw a comic strip of how you learned how to sail. Add details that will amuse readers."
- "Write a 200-word blog post about spotting a Kiwi in the New Zealand wild. Include photos."
- "Ask one of our Indonesian friends to give a brief lesson on essential words and phrases in their language. Video record the lesson, edit it and add subtitles."
- "Submit a story about sea kayaking in Thailand to an online writing contest."
- "Display and label all the currencies you collected. Calculate how much of that currency would be needed to buy a Snickers bar." (Snickers seems to be available almost everywhere.)

Teens

- "Audio interview three of our Sherpa guides about their lives in the Himalayan mountains. (Edit and add narration.) Use this as the narration for a photo slide show of our trek."
- "Make a 5-minute documentary on the importance of protecting national parks."
- "Write an article about painting classes in Italy, and submit it to your school newspaper for publishing."
- "Write a research paper on the plight of the Arctic polar bear."
- "Audio or video interview the cooking instructor about the origins of the ingredients and cooking methods unique to Senegalese culture."
- "Design a website to advertise Goa as an attractive tourist destination."
- "Write a reflection essay entitled "Why my experience in the Sumatran rainforest was so profound.""

A FEW THOUGHTS ON WRITING

There are many books and articles online dedicated to the writing process for specific age groups. This is not the book for that. What you will find below are simple tips and tricks that Sam and I found helpful in coaching our children on the road through the three main stages of writing – planning, writing, and editing. There is only so much time that a parent wants to dedicate to teaching their child while on vacation, and she wants the results to be effective, but not time consuming. That is the approach we followed.

Direct teaching

We found in the early weeks of our tour that leaving the children to plan and write assignments on their own wasted valuable time. They were easily distracted by the wonderful things going on around them and thus found the writing process tiresome. Since getting out and enjoying our tour destinations was so important to us, we wanted to limit how much time was wasted during study periods. Hence, there was a fair amount of direct coaching on better and faster ways of getting the work done, rather than suffering through time-consuming trial and error, which is normally a perfectly sound learning approach.

Thankfully, the kids were pretty receptive to our involvement, as they recognized that by adopting these researching and writing strategies their projects would be done faster and we could all head off to the beach sooner. In time, they found it increasingly easy to do assignments entirely on their own.

A few words on planning

As is the case with most writers, children as well as adults, the planning stage is the one most often neglected. This is unfortunate given how much more efficient the writing process will be if time is put aside at the beginning to brainstorm points to be included in the piece and then organized into a logical format.

If your child does not already plan his work, I suggest that you take the time to help him through this important stage. Aim to coach in a way that should enable him to eventually do it entirely on his own.

Guide his thinking by asking questions like, but not limited to:

- *What is your main objective in writing this paper? To convince? To entertain? To educate? To lead to action? To do something else?*

- *Who do you imagine your reader is?*
- *What does that reader need to understand?*
- *What are the main points you plan to cover?* (We usually aimed for three to five.)
- *What specific details or examples would you like to include?*
- *How might these points be organized in a logical order?*
- *How can you grab your reader's attention in your introduction?*
- *What would make a strong conclusion?*

A few words on writing

The freedom that comes with travel can liberate your young writer to be more creative. We certainly witnessed that in our own children, who took greater risks in their compositions because they felt less hemmed in than they did in the assessment-driven school culture they were coming from.

One day, Scout began work on a descriptive essay about her experience at Bambelela Monkey Rehabilitation Sanctuary. As is often the case when writing these kinds of assignments, she began with detailing background information about why we were there, how long we would be staying and what we were tasked to do as volunteers. It was a perfectly expected way to begin such an essay, but as this paper was intended to entertain as much as it was to educate the reader, I encouraged her to consider how she might begin the story with a *bang*.

After some careful thought and planning, she opened her narrative with a vivid and entertaining description of a troop of wild baboons crashing through the compound, screaming through the trees overhead, teeth bared, leaping across rows of corrugated rooftops, causing hundreds of vervet monkeys to scatter for cover.

She embraced the idea and rewrote the assignment so that it was situated entirely in the enclosures where she spent hours every day caring for the baby monkeys. She vividly described the unique sights, sounds and smells that surrounded her. With a small amount of encouragement, she turned what started out as a rather standard and unimaginative paper into a compelling short story.

As your child's writing coach, I recommend that you take the time to encourage her to stretch herself further in her writing, to take risks and to draw on her creative instincts.

A few words on editing

It was during the editing stage that we took our time analyzing the kids' academic work, and discussing with them every correction and suggestion. It took time and patience and, admittedly, there was occasional pushback when they felt it was taking too long. In the end, however, the effort was worth it as we saw how quickly their work improved from one assignment to the next.

Note that Sam and I avoided focusing exclusively on spelling, grammar or sentence structure, and encouraged more descriptive writing, the use of figurative language and more varied vocabulary by asking questions like:

- *How could you have written that a little more creatively?*
- *You used that word already. What other word could you use?*
- *Can you think of an analogy that would make that point more vivid?*
- *What details could you add to fill the story out?*
- *What senses could you use to describe the setting? Describe what you were seeing, hearing, smelling, tasting or feeling.*

Peer editing

Our two kids are close enough in age and writing ability to occasionally edit each other's work. This they enjoyed. To be sure, their feedback had to be consistently constructive and never critical. We noticed that through these exercises, the kids' editor's eyes were awakened to detail that they could later apply to their own work. It also gave them the opportunity to appreciate and learn from their siblings' unique writing styles.

Reflections on our son's academic writing

During our time in Africa, Declan produced three academic papers that stretched him as a writer – one on rhino poaching in South Africa, another on HIV/AIDS in Zimbabwe and the other defending science fiction literature. Knowing that he would be entering high school in a few short months, we wanted him to understand the qualitative difference between creative writing, which he was most comfortable with, and academic writing, which he was not.

Like most kids learning to write research papers, we noticed tendencies that undermined his academic success. To begin with, Declan put too little effort into researching his topics and instead substituted his own opinions for facts. Also, he regularly omitted important information while including superfluous points that had little to do with his thesis. Indeed, working out what information to include and what to omit is difficult for most writers.

We encouraged him to keep two key questions in mind:

a. *Who is your intended audience?*
   - *What messages and language would they best respond to?*

b. **What is your objective?**
- Narrative essay – *What story do you want to tell? How do you want your audience to feel, think or respond? Are you aiming to entertain your reader or something else?*
- Descriptive essay – *What details should you include to make your description interesting and informative? What words will help you do this?*
- Expository essay – *What do you want to inform your reader of? Which facts matter most?*
- Persuasive essay – *What do you want your audience to think, feel or do? What information will help you achieve that?*

During our time in South Africa, we joined in many discussions about rhino and elephant poaching. This ignited Declan's interest in writing a research paper on the topic. The director of the *Rhino Protection Trust* happened to be staying nearby at the time and she turned out to be a superb primary source for our son's research. Her input was supplemented by an impressive and highly-informative talk we attended by an actual anti-poaching squad leader. Declan also found a selection of books and websites covering the topic. Before he knew it, he had enough content for a solid research paper.

Declan determined that his imaginary audience were people sympathetic to the plight of endangered species, but had limited knowledge about the issue of poaching in South Africa. His goal was to raise awareness and to generate interest in combating the problem.

To our delight, his first draft on this challenging paper was strong. We were four months into our world tour, and Declan had done a lot of writing by then, including hours of one-on-one coaching through the writing process. There was still room for constructive feedback, but it was clear that his writing had improved by leaps and bounds since our January departure from Houston. He completed his final draft in no time flat, and it was a genuinely solid piece of work.

SAM HELPING WITH THE MEDICAL CARE OF A TRANQUILIZED BLACK RHINO. SOUTH AFRICA

Declan had turned a corner in his academic writing that I doubt he could have accomplished as quickly without the time and focus that schooling-through-travel had made possible.

ONLINE WRITING RESOURCES

Writers' clubs and competitions

One way to inspire your child to write may be to have her join an online writers' club or to participate in writing competitions. Regardless of location, young writers are able to share their work, get ideas and feel a part of a community of creative minds. And they can win prizes for their work!

Check out the *Spilling Ink* website, linked to the book by the same name, designed to help young writers get inspired and hone their skills. As for writing competitions, dozens can be found for kids and teens by simply typing in *writing contests kids/teens.*

Online grammar & vocabulary resources

If you want to use your time away to expand your child's vocabulary or improve her grammar, there are several interactive online services that can help. Over the years, our kids have benefitted from using **Spellodrome** and **SpellingCity**, both of which have a wide variety of entertaining activities that keep kids amused while growing their vocabularies. SpellingCity is probably best suited for younger ones, and Spellodrome is good for elementary and middle school kids.

Vocabulary.com and **Vocabtest.com** appeal more to our kids now that they have entered middle and high school.

To improve Declan and Scout's grammar, we found **IXL Language Arts** effective. For other options, just type in *online grammar games/practice*.

10 TAKEAWAYS

1. Coach your child through the planning process of writing by asking questions about the objective of the piece, her imagined readers/viewers, and key details to fill it out.

2. Encourage your child to take creative chances with his writing rather than sticking to tried and tested patterns and vocabulary.

3. Don't limit your coaching to grammar and spelling. Encourage your child to explore new vocabulary and to use figurative language.

4. To add variety to the learning process, introduce peer editing. This will help both children develop their editing and proofreading skills while learning from each other's writing.

5. Explore online writing resources well in advance of your journey so you don't need to waste valuable travel time doing it.

6. Make journaling and creative writing regular family activities during relaxation periods.

7. Encourage family members to share their creative writing.

8. Avoid editing or offering constructive feedback on journal entries or creative writing as it might discourage

free expression. Stick closely to the philosophy that the more your child writes, the better his skills will become.

9. Involve your child in identifying academic writing topics that interest her.

10. Keep the learning process interesting by being creative about the types of assignments your child works on: Essays, articles, PowerPoint presentations (including voiceover), brochures, video documentaries, pictures, interviews, writing contests, blog posts and more.

Chapter 7
MATH

Before leaving Houston, we signed up and paid for an accredited online math program that looked like it ticked all the boxes. I had gone through the course descriptions to confirm that the requisite skills were covered and then had them approved by the kids' current math teachers. These were helpful meetings as both of our kids' teachers clarified exactly which skills would be critical the following academic year.

Within a few days on the road, however, it had become abundantly clear that the chosen math curricula were poorly designed and that the kids were not benefiting from them. I canceled the programs, arranged for refunds, and had the kids switch over to Khan Academy. (See Sal Khan's presentation on ***Ted.com*** for an overview of the program.) Scout signed on to do 7th Grade US Math and Declan, Pre-Algebra.

We opted to have the kids cover the entire years' content, rather than cherry-pick specific topics they would miss during their absence from school. This proved to be a wise decision. They moved along at a steady pace, and had established a solid foundation from which to re-enter school the following year. Since Scout's teacher had stressed the importance of geometry and graphing in our pre-departure meeting, we supplemented those topics with online *IXL Math* practice exercises.

Within seven short weeks, Declan had *mastered* 100% of Pre-Algebra, and was free to move onto Algebra. The boost in his confidence was palpable. This was, admittedly, followed by a period of resistance about moving onto the next level, but we were adamant that he keep the momentum going. Eventually, he gave in and mastered 25% of algebra that he would soon cover in 9th grade, which gave him an edge when he returned to school.

Sam and I breathed easier knowing that rather than falling behind in their studies due to our choice to travel, in some ways the kids actually learned more, faster, than they would have at school.

ADDITIONAL MATH RESOURCES

As discussed earlier, having consistent, high-quality internet access is needed for any online program. As this cannot always be counted on when you're traveling, I came prepared with Kindle-version SSAT and ISEE exam questions that I downloaded for free.

Another easy, be it bulkier, option would have been to bring along a PSAT, SSAT, SAT or ISEE study guide that included lessons and practice tests. These handy guides provide quality instructions to math problems common on standardized tests.

5 TAKEAWAYS

1. Determine in advance which mathematical skills your child will need when he returns to school and make sure those are covered in the curriculum you choose.

2. Explore the many online math resources available, including complete academic-year curricula and supplementary exercises.

3. When considering a fee-based online program, make sure it provides a money back guarantee.

4. Bring additional math resources that don't require WIFI, in case internet access is interrupted.

5. Begin your search by looking through the Khan Academy program.

Chapter 8
SCIENCE

Our children's science curricula were perhaps the most difficult to organize because, while we needed to ensure that the kids had the necessary prerequisites to progress in their subjects, we also wanted to allow them time and freedom to explore their own interests.

We initially signed up with the same online school we had chosen for math, but the science program turned out to be equally boring and ineffective, so we dropped it after a couple of days and got our money refunded. This was Sam's cue to shift into science teacher mode and draw up a learning strategy that would take Scout through the physical geography topics she would be missing at school, as will be discussed below. He already had a pretty solid understanding of the topics, and he managed to find an impressive assortment of supplementary resources online.

For Declan, we made the rather radical decision to allow him to run with his own interests in science rather than have him follow a set program.

Self-directed learning

Our son had shown a genuine interest in astronomy for years but never had enough time to explore it during the regular school term. These months away were his chance. With a fervency he had never shown his studies before, he dove into the subject matter. Hours were spent searching through online videos and articles. Not only was he able to cover a wide variety of topic - black holes, Apollo landings,

NASA programs, the International Space Station - but because he was so interested in the subject, he retained it at a far greater depth than I had ever witnessed in him before.

In no time flat, his areas of interest crept into other subjects, which is so often the case with online learning. A trail was created from one topic to the next. He learned about how solar energy was harnessed, about quantum computers, even the immune system and the spread of disease became curiosities for him.

Soon he began to identify his favorite online learning producers, such as Kurzgesagt, whom our son came to refer to as *"That Really Interesting Guy"*, because of the familiar voice of the narrator. He was hooked from the first film he watched called *Everything You Need to Know About Planet Earth*. In a matter of weeks, he had watched all of Kurzgesagt's YouTube science videos, as well as others on the Syrian refugee crisis, debunking conspiracy theories, the stock exchange, the banking crisis, the *War on Drugs*, and the overuse of antibiotics.

To supplement his learning, Declan had online subscriptions to *Wired* and *Popular Science* magazines which he and Sam shared. Many of the articles became catalysts for interesting dinner conversations, which invariably drew Scout and me in.

What If! is a website and book by the same title, created by NASA Robotics Engineer, Randal Monroe. It brought Declan hours of entertainment (and learning) as he explored hypothetical questions in science.

By the end, the impressive volume of content Declan learned about science (and by extension, many other subjects) over those months proved to me without a doubt that self-directed learning can be more powerful than traditional classroom learning, for some children.

Following a science curriculum

Despite Declan having learned so much about a wide range of science topics on his own, we needed to ensure that he covered the essentials of chemistry and physics. Scout, moreover, had to learn about plate tectonics, volcanoes, and meteorology. This was where talking with the kids' science teachers was critical. Both of our kids' teachers were extremely generous during our pre-departure meetings, clearly outlining the topics that would be covered in their absences.

Knowing specifically what they needed to learn, we and the kids scrolled through dozens of websites, including Khan Academy and YouTube videos, to find content that covered those areas. We took the time to discuss the content together and developed assignments designed to confirm the kids' understanding.

Learning in the field

GEOTHERMAL ENERGY
NEW ZEALAND

Our approach to teaching our daughter science was very different from Declan's self-directed approach. Sam was raised in a national park in Aotearoa, the Maori name for New Zealand. Literally translated, the word means *land of the long white cloud*. From an early age, his parents taught him about the natural world – the local flora, fauna, geology, wind directions and, as you'd expect, clouds. Is it any wonder that we felt that New Zealand was the ideal location for Scout to launch her meteorology and physical geography studies?

Sam gave Scout the ideal learning experience by explaining the what, where, why, when and how of the clouds over our heads. He then moved on to teach her about plate tectonics, in his home country where evidence of seismic activity surrounded us daily - geysers, volcanoes, and earthquake fault lines. He continued this education in Namibia, where the unusual, and spectacular, landscape provided even more evidence of geological transformation, bringing our daughter once again in direct contact with the science topics she was studying.

NAMIB DESERT
NAMIBIA

While learning how to kiteboard in the Philippines, Sam expanded Scout's learning in meteorology to seasonal wind directions and currents. This blended smoothly into lessons about other types of weather patterns, including hurricanes and tornadoes, which are an annual occurrence in the archipelago.

Wildlife studies

Our entire family's ultimate experiential science education took place in Africa, where we learned hands-on at Bambelela Monkey Sanctuary about rehabilitating primates for their eventual release back into the wild. We learned about their diets, social structures, communication systems, mating behaviors and so much more.

With Siyafunda Conservation, in South Africa, we collected data for use in academic research. This gave us incredible opportunities to observe abundant wildlife, gaining insight into different animals' diets, predator-prey relationships, survival traits and behaviors, and the fragile ecosystem in which they struggle to survive.

I recall one evening in South Africa our game ranger pointed to a kettle of vultures circle in the distant sky. It was indicative of a dead animal in the bush below. *"They will clean up the remains of the carcass. Without them, the remains would rot and disease would spread."* Days later, in a discussion with an anti-rhino poaching activist, we learned that poachers had taken to poisoning the meat of the rhinos they had just killed so that vultures that followed would die and thus not alert their anti-poaching foes. This gruesome strategy was resulting in fewer vultures in Southern Africa's game reserves, leading to the spread of disease throughout the ecosystem.

We learned that sad reality on the back of a Land Rover in the South African bush, not out of the pages of a textbook. And as such, I doubt the kids will ever forget it.

A RATHER LUCKY DAY OF WILDLIFE VIEWING AT ETOSHA NATIONAL PARK. JUST US AND THE ANIMALS.
NAMIBIA

4 TAKEAWAYS

1. Get input from your child's school about the science topics she'll miss and will need in preparation to move ahead in the subject. Base most of your plan around that, allowing room for exceptional learning opportunities found along your travel route.

2. If possible, build science study directly into your gap year locations. Geography, geology, meteorology, botany, ornithology, astronomy, marine biology and animal science are some of the topics that can be observed in the field.

3. Self-directed learning is when a student explores a topic of interest, and he directs the process himself. A gap year is the ideal time to introduce this type of learning.

4. Take advantage of the impressive array of online resources available for learners today – from pre-school right up to university level courses, by some of the world's most influential learning institutions. Many options are free.

Chapter 9
ASSESSMENT

As I explained earlier, the goal of the schooling-through-travel methodology is to educate, not to evaluate. We wanted to create a system unlike the teach-to-the-test approach our kids were falling victim to in school, that stressed grades before actual understanding. Our objective was quite the opposite – for our kids to develop a greater appreciation of the world, and a craving to learn more about it.

There's little doubt in our minds that we achieved this goal through the combination of what the kids were exposed to on the trip, and their complementary assignments and readings. Their intellectual growth over those months was palpable.

This was most obviously the case in their studies of social studies and English, but even in science we witnessed it, particularly in Declan. He may not have learned how to recite the order of the periodic table as though he had been cramming for a mid-term exam, but the breadth and depth of his understanding and enthusiasm for such a wide range of scientific theories and topics through his self-directed learning can only be described as a genuine *education*.

Thus, during our family gap year, assessment was merely a gentle tool used to guide the kids' studies and to identify gaps that might still need filling.

ASSESSMENT

No grades were given for the kids' work. In fact, I question whether giving grades would have somehow stalled the learning process by externalizing their motivation. If a child knows, for instance, that her paper is going to be ranked on a scale of one to a hundred, then where will her thinking go? Her goal will shift away from wanting to explore the topic, to wanting to impress the assessor. This fundamentally goes against what we wanted to instill in the children – that learning is pleasurable, perhaps challenging, but always satisfying, in its own right.

Assessment through conversation

Spending all day, every day, together for months allows so much time for family interaction - one of the true benefits of a family gap year. As we only had two children with us, not a crowded classroom of 30 to 40 students, we were in the fortunate position of being able to gauge how much they had learned about particular topics simply through regular conversation. We found ourselves talking over dinner about climate change and droughts in Southern Africa, space research and the merits of reintroducing the kiwi into New Zealand's national forests; about differences and similarities in the cultures we were visiting in South-East Asia and the plight of Laos' desperately poor hill tribes. When your 12 and 13-year old can keep up in those conversations, you know they're learning something.

Questions like the ones below encouraged our kids to reveal what they were learning:

- *What was your favorite thing about that experience?*
- *What do you think about what happened/you saw today?*
- *What did you learn that you didn't know before?*

- *How can you imagine it being done differently somewhere else?*
- *What leads you to that impression?*
- *How does this compare with what you've seen elsewhere?*
- *What did you like? What did you not like? What's your reasoning behind that?*
- *What would you like to know more about?*
- *What will you do differently next time?*

You'll notice that the questions above begin with either "how" or "what". This is a trick I learned through my executive coaching practice. Open questions that begin with these words stimulate discussion. Words like "do" or "why", on the other hand, can put respondents on the defensive, or result in simple yes or no answers.

Assessment through writing

As has been described in detail in preceding pages, the children's knowledge grew as they researched and composed written assignments, and their level of understanding shone through in their work. What was also evident was how their skills in research, analysis, and writing progressed from one project to the next.

Sam and I made sure that every assignment was thoroughly read through and discussed. In that context, it was not difficult to work out what was sinking in, what was still unclear, and what additional learning might be advantageous.

MATH ASSESSMENT

Math is different. Continuous assessment helps to ensure that the foundation is solid before the learner moves on to the next topic.

Khan Academy

The Khan Academy math curricula, which we used for both of our kids, requires that the student masters a skill before moving up to the next level. Through easy-to-follow videos, skills are taught in a logical sequence. The system assesses the child's ability to apply the skills to progressively more difficult problems.

Unlike many traditional school settings, in which a child is moved up regardless of how well she understands the concept – a 70% grade, for instance, will still enable the child to move to the next level - the Khan Academy online program continuously assesses the child until she gets five correct answers in a row, thus earning her the *Mastered* designation. At that point, the next skill in the series is introduced.

The continuous assessment feature enabled our kids to progress at their own pace, and return to videos and explanations whenever they were having difficulty. And the recognition awards built into the assessment system kept them motivated.

A similar format is found in the online IXL math program, which our kids turned to when they wanted a brief change from Khan Academy. The student chooses a specific topic to work through in a series of increasingly challenging questions. Points are earned for each correct answer in that topic, and for each incorrect answer, points are lost. A brief lesson follows each incorrect answer so the student can see where she went wrong and how to do it correctly the next time. The process continues until 100 points are earned, and thus the student is assumed to have mastered the skill.

Standardized Test-Prep Books

You may have seen books used by students to prepare for standardized tests, like the PST, SSAT, SAT, and ISEE. These books include lessons and practice tests and can be used as an alternative to a traditional math textbook.

Our kids first used these books when they were preparing to sit the ISEE entry exam required by US private schools. The practice tests helped us identify the skills the kids needed to work on, and we found the explanations contained inside easy to understand.

These books can be found at most bookstores. Alternatively, scroll through vendor websites where the books are sold online to get a sense of additional services available, including free and fee-based online testing tools.

SCIENCE

Scout studied the list of topics suggested by her school's science teacher, and then completed an assignment that her father designed to confirm her understanding of the key learning points.

After studying volcanoes and other seismic phenomena, she produced a PowerPoint presentation, which included a series of questions and answers such as:

1. *What is a caldera? A caldera is . . . .*
2. *What causes a tsunami? A tsunami is caused by . . . .*

For her study of the Earth's structure and weather systems, she completed a test that Sam drew up that included questions like:

1. *Draw a diagram of Earth's layers and label them.*
2. *What is the mantle made of?*

FAMILY TRIVIA GAME

Sam and I wanted to make sure that we remembered as much as we could about each place we visited, so I designed a trivia game that included facts gathered along the way. It turned out to be as much fun as it was educational; brought out during mealtimes, when it was too hot to go out into the tropical afternoon heat, or on long drives.

The questions and answers came from information shared by our guides and local people we met, *Lonely Planet* guides, museums visited, local newspapers and the Country Facts Sheets the kids wrote up for each place we visited. The list of questions was updated daily.

Sample questions:

37. How do you say *thank you* in Lao?

    khob chai

105. What is the approximate population of the Philippines?

    100 million

201. What is the currency of Vietnam?

    Dong

349. What is the name of head monkey in a troupe? And what gender is the head?

    Alpha, female

5 TAKEAWAYS

1. Try to limit testing that might simply distract your child from the experiential learning that comes with travel.

2. Regular family discussions and written assignments should give you a strong indication of what your child has learnt about the places visited during the tour.

3. Checking understanding of topics in science can be helpful in ensuring that your child has the prerequisites needed to move forward in the subject. This may be done through a written quiz that you create, or through verbal questions and answers. There are also free online quizzes covering the essentials of a range of topics.

4. Math is one subject that requires continuous assessment since a child needs a solid foundation before he can take on more challenging concepts. There are excellent tools, like Khan Academy, IXL and standardized test prep books that can help with this.

5. Design your own *Family Trivia Game* using information gathered about the places you visited and people you've met. It's a game and assessment tool all in one.

Chapter 10
THE RESISTANT CHILD

No child is going to be entirely, or consistently, committed to studying when there are many interesting distractions around them; and this is only compounded when traveling. So, what will you do when your child complains that she'd rather go to the beach than complete her math lesson? How will you respond when your son refuses to study any more science because he's *"on vacation"*? Will you give in, be flexible or hold firm? The onus falls on you as the parent-teacher to get things back on track, and it requires focus, effective communication and a high degree of willpower.

Clarify your terms & conditions

We found that a combination of pressure and flexibility worked in making our kids buy into the process. Months before departure, we began a candid conversation with the kids about what we were planning and their roles in making it work. They recognized that during those months of travel they would be freed from eight hours of traditional classroom learning a day, plus two to three hours of homework per evening, IF they agreed to our terms and conditions.

Given that, Declan and Scout agreed to approximately two to three hours of studying per day on average, without complaint. (This may sound like a lot but keep in mind that reading and writing were their evening entertainment.) They agreed to accept us as their teachers during those hours (and not to take advantage of the fact that we were their parents) and respect the assignments we agreed upon. Finally, they were to approach their work with enthusiasm, energy, and efficiency so that the entire family could be released more quickly to enjoy our holiday.

Some parents might want to put this agreement in writing, but we did not feel it necessary as our two kids were clearly on board.

Be sensitive to energy levels

Once our travels were underway, we made sure to be sensitive to the kids' energy levels when deciding what and when to study. We took time to observe when each child was more receptive to learning – be it in the morning after a refreshing sleep, after a long day of fresh air and exercise, or in the evening once the heat of the day had worn off - and tried to schedule their studies accordingly. We had learned the hard way, years before, that forcing the kids to do work that requires concentration when they are tired will only make them resent the work and their teachers.

Instead, we tended toward using high-energy periods for math and science work, and lazier periods for reading, writing, video editing and other creative work. When the kids asked to opt out of a session because they were tired, they had to back it up with a commitment to another time in the near future. *I am too tired to do this math right now, but I promise to return to it at 11:30 am. I'll read now, instead.*

We also made sure that the kids' diets were conducive to learning. A lot of healthy protein in the morning and for snacks, rather than bread or pancakes, helped to keep them energized for much of the day.

> **MANAGING RESTRICTED DIETS ON THE ROAD**
>
> *My friend, Erica, has had food allergies for years and has advice about how they can be managed on the road. This can be helpful for parents who worry that their kids' learning will be impacted by not eating right.*
>
> *Do your research and know what's available in the places you're traveling to, particularly the staples. We try to stay in places where we have our own kitchen so I can cook what I need. I'll bring food with me that's easy to carry.*
>
> *When touring the US and Australia, we bring a cooler filled with foods I can eat. I have also been known to bring a thermos full of stew onto a flight – and was lucky enough not be stopped by security. [Depending on your allergies, you may be able to have special meals provided by the airline, particularly on international flights.]*
>
> *With that in mind, it's worth remembering that most cities today have modern, well-stocked supermarkets. We were generally impressed by the quality of food we found virtually everywhere we went on our world tour, including cities and towns in developing countries.*
>
> *If your or your child has specific dietary requirements, do your research in advance to learn what is available where you're going.*

Get the kids involved in choosing assignments

Our kids were invited to come up with assignment ideas that motivated them. Often we would bounce ideas around during long drives and over meals, making sure that their opinions were respected and regularly incorporated into the curricula.

One morning, Scout came up with the idea of writing about her experience on our favorite snorkeling reef in the Philippines, using her five senses in her description. It was a technique she learned weeks earlier in New Zealand. Sam and I, of course, encouraged her idea as it made so much sense to write a creative piece about such a full-on sensory adventure, from the warmth of the sun on her back to the gentle sway of the water's current, to the colorful fish and coral that surrounded her and the taste of the salty water. Her final piece was as much poem as it was a journal, and we recognized it as yet another stage in her growth as a writer.

With each assignment, we discussed the learning objectives and justification for including it in their portfolios. As time progressed, Declan and Scout were able to pinpoint what made a worthy assignment and what elements should be included to give it academic heft, like a clear structure, solid research, significant detail and good writing.

SHOOTING AN ARROW, SAN BUSHMAN STYLE, IS FAR MORE DIFFICULT THAN IT LOOKS.
NAMIBIA

Pair & Group work

After weeks of struggling with poor internet access in New Zealand and the Philippines, the kids needed to make some serious progress in Singapore in their online math program before we headed to Africa. They worked hard initially, but as their enthusiasm began to wane we invited them to work together on some math problems. These were simple algebraic questions that overlapped in their two math curricula. The teamwork proved to be a fun alternative. They attempted each question individually before comparing answers, and when their answers differed they would work on them together until their solutions matched. They enjoyed the competitive challenge of getting the right answer and having a chance to teach the other what they knew. Although this would not have worked as a permanent method of getting through the math curricula, it was a welcome change.

Cooperative learning like this can be done in many subjects. As was discussed earlier, the kids got a real kick out of editing each other's written work.

Producing videos are ideal for group work. Interviewing each other, sharing and editing photos, adding music and voiceover can be great fun when done together.

Dealing with push-back

Despite how well we thought things were going, Scout started giving us some serious pushback at about three months into the trip. While Declan was moving full-steam ahead in most subjects, Scout, who is generally a very active and social child, was becoming easily distracted. She began reading and writing less, and was not producing consistently solid work. We found that she would often look busy but was in fact doing very little.

Then we noticed that passive-aggressive behaviors began to creep in with both kids, like "forgetting" to charge their computers or Kindles the evening before, meaning less could be accomplished in the morning.

How we finally chose to tackle this problem was pretty straightforward. We introduced specific project deadlines, tied to clear rewards (and punishments), which were then closely monitored.

- *"If you complete the assignment by 3PM, then you will be free to use the iPad on the plane."*
- *"If you edit the assignment to the best of your ability by noon, and I am satisfied with it, then you can stop. Otherwise, you'll continue working on it after lunch."*
- *"If you complete 5% of the math curriculum by Tuesday then you can watch TV at the hotel in Johannesburg."*

This last incentive may sound like a small reward for a lot of work, but for our kids, who had gone screen-free for weeks, it proved to be an effective motivator.

5 TAKEAWAYS

1. Before departure, clarify the terms and conditions of your road schooling plan with your child and get her agreement.

2. Be sensitive to your child's energy levels during study times, giving more challenging work during high-energy periods, and more relaxing creative work, reading and writing during low energy times.

3. Invite your child to help choose assignments that interest him.

4. For variety, include occasional group work activities.

5. When all else fails, state your requirements clearly with meaningful consequences.

Chapter 11
THE POST-TOUR REPORT

The kids' learning activities were tracked using the table explained in Chapter 3. When we returned to the US, this content was organized into a report for each child to present to administrators at their current and future schools.

Here is a summary of Declan's report, covering 8-months of study.

WORLD TOUR LEARNING REPORT

Declan Ash-Dale

SOCIAL STUDIES & ENGLISH

VIETNAM

Our family's tour of southern Vietnam focused primarily on the history and culture of the Mekong Delta region. We learned about the Vietnamese-American War from the Vietnamese perspective, post-war Vietnam, current lifestyles of those in urban and rural areas, including housing, food, family, and education.

CAN THO WATER MARKET

Projects completed:

- Narrated PowerPoint presentation: *American & Vietnamese War from the Vietnamese Perspective*
- Journal: *My Vietnam*
- Creative writing: *A Vietnamese Massage*
- Vietnam Facts Sheet
- Vietnam Trivia Game

Extracurricular Activities:

- Tour of a floating water-market, Mekong Delta
- Tour of American- Vietnam War Museum, Ho Chi Minh
- Tour of Cu Chi Tunnels, Ho Chi Minh
- Vietnamese Cuisine Tour, Can Tho
- Tour of rice and noodle making factories, Can Tho
- Daily cycling around the region to observe and experience local life

LAOS

Our tour of Laos focused primarily on Lao Buddhism and the lives of hill tribes people, particularly the Hmong. We also learned about the bombing of Laos by the US during the Vietnam War, the long-term effects of the war and the subsequent role of Communism in the country. We took classes in Lao cuisine, arts and crafts, and got familiarized with the influence of the colonial French on the culture and architecture. Finally, we witnessed first-hand how Lao people today work to survive below the poverty line.

EARLY MORNING ALMS GIVING CEREMONY

Projects completed:

- *Trip Advisor Review: The Mistreatment of Elephants in Laos' Tourism Industry*
- Creative writing/essay: *I am a Monk* – a first-person creative story on being a Buddhist monk in Laos, including facts learned from an actual monk
- *My days in Laos* - Journal
- Laos Facts Sheet
- Laos Trivia Game
- Creative writing: *The German Spy*

Extracurricular Activities:

- Lao cooking class, Luang Prabang

- *Elephant Experience*, Luang Prabang
- Private tutorial on meditation, Buddhism and Lao monastic life by senior Lao monk, Muang Ngoi
- Weaving course led by a Hmong hill tribeswoman

NEW ZEALAND

In New Zealand, our family visited several national parks where we learned about the country's unique flora and fauna, as well as active volcanic and geothermal geology.

Projects Completed:

- Brochure project- *New Zealand Through the Senses*. A series of short articles about tourist sites visited in NZ:
    - Opito Bay
    - Waitomo Caves
    - Whitewater Rafting
    - Thermal New Zealand
    - Sea Kayaking at Abel Tasman National Park
    - Tramping through Abel Tasman National Park
    - Lake Rotoiti (Nelson Lakes National Park)
- New Zealand Facts Sheet
- New Zealand Trivia Game
- Creative writing: *The Englishman*

KAYAKING THE NEW ZEALAND COAST

Extracurricular Activities:

- Campervanning tour of New Zealand's North and South Islands
- Caving, exploring underground glow worms, stalactites and stalagmites
- Visiting a site of volcanic activity – mud pools and geysers
- Visiting National Volcano Museum – site of the largest volcanic explosion
- White water rafting
- Sea kayaking along Abel Tasman National Park

PHILIPPINES

Our visit to the Philippines took us to Boracay, where we learned to kiteboard, and then to a remote island far off the beaten tourist track named Tablas. We developed friendships with local fishermen, farmers, builders and their families;

learned their games, ate their food and experienced life in grass huts under coconut palms.

LEARNING A LOCAL GAME WITH A GROUP OF NEW FRIENDS. PHILIPPINES

Projects Completed:

- Essay Project: *Biography of a Family on Tablas Island*
- Essay: *An Argument in Favor of Science Fiction Literature*
- Philippines Facts Page
- Philippines Trivia Game
- Creative writing: *Andromeda* – A science fiction novel (18,000 words)

SOUTH AFRICA

Our visit to South Africa was an intensive African wildlife experience. For two-weeks my family and I spent volunteering at Bambelela Monkey Rehabilitation Sanctuary, where we worked directly with baboons and vervet monkeys to help prepare them to return to the wild. The latter part of our stay had us volunteering for Siyafunda Wildlife Conservation, where we collected data on wildlife in the "Big Five" Makalali Game Reserve. (The data was then shared with the World Wildlife Fund, and used by university postgraduate students in the US and UK.) We learned about conservation and anti-poaching efforts in the Limpopo region. On our final day, we were actively involved in an operation to save a tranquilized black rhino in the bush.

Projects Completed:

- Essay: *Anti Rhino Poaching in South Africa*
- Essay/Journal Project – *A Rhino Rescue in South Africa*
- Video documentary: *Voluntourism in South Africa* – drawing from experiences at Bambelela & Makalali
- South Africa Facts Sheet
- South Africa Trivia Game

Extracurricular activities:

- Worked to rehabilitate vervet monkeys and baboons
- Collected and collated data on wildlife at Makalali Wildlife Reserve
- Toured a crocodile farm, Limpopo, South Africa
- Went on a game drive – Zebula Game Reserve

- Viewed a presentation called *How to Survive Against African's Big Five*
- *Attended a presentation called Anti-Rhino Poaching Efforts in South Africa, by K9 Anti-Poaching Squad*

NAMIBIA

Our self-driving tour of Namibia enabled us to experience Namibia's unique landscape, wildlife and indigenous tribes. During the journey, we visited the world's oldest desert, the Namib, were welcomed into the homes of Himba and San Bushman tribes, attended a Herero wedding, and viewed an extensive variety of wildlife at Etosha National Park.

Projects Completed:

- Pamphlet: *Etosha National Animal Reserve*
- Journal/essay: *My Attendance at a Herero Wedding*
- Journal/essay: *My Visit to a Himba Village*
- Journal/essay: *My Visit San Bushmen of the Kalahari*

Extracurricular Activities:

- Camped atop a 4x4 from central to northern Namibia
- Viewed wildlife (day and night) at Etosha National Reserve
- Attended a traditional Herero tribal wedding
- Visited a traditional Himba village
- Spent a day in a San Bushman tribal village – learned about hunting and gathering traditions, herbs for medicinal and hunting purposes, archery and fire-starting skills, and participated in tribal dances

HAVING SUCH FUN WITH HIMBA CHILDREN.

ZIMBABWE

Our visit was spent in Victoria Falls, where we enjoyed views of the falls and cruised along the Zambezi River that separates Zimbabwe and Zambia. We taught English at several pre and primary schools, helped at a garden for and by victims of HIV/AIDS, and at a home for elderly people. We were also given a private tour of a lion conservation project, which included walking four lion cubs through the bush.

Projects Completed:

- Essay: *Zimbabwe's Struggle with HIV/AIDS*
- Video: *Community Volunteering in Zimbabwe*

Extracurricular Activities

- Taught English at Chino Timba Preschool
- Taught English at Chino Timba Primary School

- Taught English at Rose of Charity Orphanage
- Taught English at His Grace Rural Preschool
- Helped at the garden for people with HIV/AIDS
- Did maintenance work at Chino Timba Old Folks Home
- Cruised the Zambezi River between Zimbabwe and Zambia (and spotted hippos)

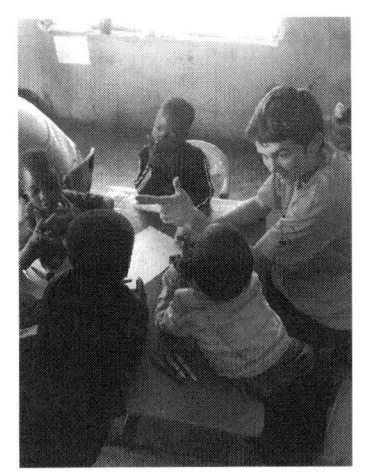

TEACHING MATH AT GRACE SCHOOL ZIMBABWE

- Attended a private tutorial on lion conservation and went on a lion walk
- Visited an Ndebele village where we were taught farming and cooking practices, how to carry water buckets on our heads, and enjoyed traditional dancing
- Attended two African church services

SCIENCE

Most of Declan's study in science was self-directed. He researched topics of interest to him by accessing a wide variety of online resources. Here is the list of documentaries he watched and discussed with his family.

- *What is Life? Is Death Real?*
- *The Last Star in the Universe – Red Dwarfs Explained*
- *Why the War on Drugs is a Huge Failure*

- *The Antibiotic Apocalypse*
- *The Fermi Paradox (Part I & II)*
- *Addiction*
- *The Immune System – Bacteria Infection*
- *The History and Future of Time and Everything*
- *Black Holes Explained*
- *Why Ebola is so dangerous?*
- *Three Ways to Destroy the Universe*
- *Are you alone in the universe?*
- *What if there was a black hole in your pocket?*
- *Fracking Explained: Opportunity or Danger*
- *How Nuclear Energy Works*
- *Three Reasons Why Nuclear Energy is Terrible*
- *Three Reasons Why Nuclear Energy is Awesome*
- *What is light?*
- *What is dark matter and dark energy?*
- *Measles Explained*
- *Everything You Need to Know About Planet Earth*
- *Atoms as Big as Mountains – Neutron Stars Explained*
- *The Big Bang – the Beginning of Everything*
- *The Solar System – Our Home in Space*
- *Quantum Computers*
- *How big is the moon, really?*
- *Moons of Mars Explained*
- *The Moons of Pluto Explained*
- *How to Catch a Dwarf Planet*

- *Atoms Explained*
- *Top Ten Facts – Space 1, 2, 3, 4, 5, 6*
- *The Space Elevator*
- *Top 10 Facts – Earth*
- *The Antibiotic Apocalypse*
- *The Last Star in the Universe*
- *The History and Future of Everything*

African wildlife conservation was another area of study we learned first-hand:

- Biodiversity data collection and animal behavior study (Siyafunda Conservation, South Africa)
- Primate Rehabilitation – cared for vervet monkeys and baboons for rehabilitation back into the wild (Bambelela Monkey Sanctuary, South Africa)

MATH

Math study completed:

- Khan Academy – Pre-Algebra 100% mastered
- Khan Academy – Algebra 25% mastered
- IXL - Grade 8 – supplementary study

READING

The books Declan read during the tour were:

- *The Martian*, by Andy Weir
- *What if*, by Randall Monroe
- *The Elephant Whisperer*, by Lawrence Anthony

- *2001: A Space Odyssey*, Arthur C. Clarke
- *Gravity*, by Tess Gerritsen
- *2010: A Space Odyssey*, by Arthur C. Clarke
- *Whatever you do, don't run! True Tales of a Botswana Safari Guide*, by Peter Allison
- *Do your ears pop in space?*, by Mark Mulane
- *A Long Walk to Water*, by Linda Sue Park
- *I am Malia*, by Christina Lamb and Malala Yousafzai
- *Kruger Tales*, Jeff Gordon
- *Born Free*, Joy Adamson
- *Nightingale*, Kristin Hannah
- *Into Thin Air*, Jon Krakauer

AUDIOBOOKS

The audiobooks Declan completed during the tour were:

- *Murder on the Orient Express*, by Agatha Christy
- *The Prince & the Pauper*, Mark Twain
- *Harry Potter & the Philosopher's Stone*, by J.K. Rowling
- *Harry Potter & the Chamber of Secrets*, by J.K. Rowling
- *Harry Potter & the Prisoner of Azkaban*, by J.K. Rowling
- *Harry Potter & the Goblet of Fire*, by J.K. Rowling
- *Harry Potter & the Order of the Phoenix*, JK Rowling

CONCLUSION

So, that's how we schooled our children through travel – from beginning to end. The kids advanced to their next grade levels when we returned to Houston, and their results proved that they had not lost any ground due to our taking them out of school for several months. Declan's confidence had blossomed by the time we got back and he approached his school work with more enthusiasm than he had ever shown before. Scout had kept up academically, and she had become noticeably more self-reliant.

Where she struggled was in her motivation and social circle. Our months of continuous change and stimulation had energized our girl, but that came to an abrupt halt the minute we landed back in Houston. It took time to get over how *"boring"* everything had become – her classes, her teachers and even her friends. She pined for Africa.

But this dip didn't last. Within months, we had relocated to Boston, where her attention shifted to her new environment, new school and new friends, while holding firmly to her plans of relocating to Africa after university.

Would we do it again? Yes. Even if the kids were already in high school? Yes. In fact, we are in discussions now about the possibly of taking Scout away one more time, during her final year of high school. It might cause a minor disruption in her college entrance, but it's a minor price to pay for doing the thing we love most – travel. We've done our research and there are good universities in our home country of Canada that would accept completion of required courses for high school graduation (which she can do online), a solid showing on the SAT exam, a transcript showing strong marks in 10th and 11th Grades, and a portfolio similar to the one she created on this trip.

If that is the route we decide to take, we'll do so after Declan has graduated from high school here in Boston, as he is keen to pursue classes in genetics and astronomy, and would prefer to study alongside likeminded science enthusiasts.

Sam and I are thoroughly enjoying our new life in Boston, but long for the days when we can return to the road. But it will never be quite the same as those precious months when the world first became our children's classroom.

ABOUT THE AUTHOR

Taryn Ash grew up in Canada, and spent most of her adult life living, studying, working and raising a family between Japan, Singapore and China, before relocating to the US in 2013. She started out as a high school teacher in Japan, before becoming a college lecturer in Singapore, and then a training and development consultant and corporate learning curriculum designer. She continues to be a stakeholder in a tutoring center in China, while running an executive coaching practice in Boston, for local and overseas clients. Travel remains Taryn's greatest passion, having visited close to 50 countries to date, with plans underway to visit the next 50.

Also Featured in this Book

Sam Dale was born and raised in New Zealand, before relocating to Asia, where he met and married Taryn. He started out as a journalist before directing his attention to the energy consulting industry. He is a passionate musician, sportsman and rugby fan. He is now working on plans to eventually return to Africa with Taryn, in the hopes of helping to bring renewable energy and clean water to communities who need it.

Scout Dawson Ash-Dale is an athlete, dancer and animal lover. She dreams of studying psychology at university, before earning a degree in education and development studies so she can run schools in Africa.

Declan Courtenay Ash-Dale is fascinated by history and world events, technology and science. He dreams of studying genetics at university and of becoming a technology entrepreneur while making his home in Whistler, Canada.

Did you find this book helpful?

If you enjoyed this book, please let other readers know by sharing your experience on Amazon.com.

If you have feedback that could help me make the book more helpful to future readers, please contact me through www.familygapyears.com

Happy travels!

Taryn

Another Book by Taryn Ash

Available on Amazon.com

This book is written specially for parents who long to discover the world with their kids, but are overwhelmed by seemingly insurmountable logistical, financial and emotional obstacles. It offers recommendations, advice and answers to questions, from how to design the ideal itinerary to match your budget, to how to have your home and pets cared for in your absence. Peppered throughout this book are anecdotes from the author's personal experiences. You will also find words of wisdom from other well-traveled parents who have made exploring the world an integral feature of their families' lives.

Taryn Ash, her husband, Sam and two kids, Declan and Scout, put their comfortable lives in the U.S. on hold for several glorious months, to embark on a life-affirming tour of 12 countries on four continents.

Together they camped atop a 4x4 in the Namibian desert, ate spicy cobra in Vietnam, taught English to enthusiastic youngsters in Zimbabwe, and earned blisters on their hands restoring a medieval fortress wall in southern France. They hunted for tropical shells with local children on a remote Philippine island, worked hands-on to rehabilitate monkeys and baboons in South Africa, and collected data on African wildlife for academic research. They splashed their ways through pitch-black tunnels speckled with florescent glow worms in New Zealand, practiced Buddhist chant under the tutelage of a wise monk in rural Laos, and learned to kite board through the winds of the South China Sea. And that's not all.

This book was written with the sole purpose of helping adventure-minded parents to finally *grab the kids and go.*

Printed in Great Britain
by Amazon